3·95

WOMEN AND THE FAMILY

WOMEN AND WORLD DEVELOPMENT SERIES

This series has been developed by the **UN-NGO Group on Women and Development** and makes available the most recent information, debate and action being taken on world development issues, and the impact on women. Each volume is fully illustrated and attractively presented. Each outlines its particular subject, as well as including an introduction to resources and guidance on how to use the books in workshops and seminars. The aim of each title is to bring women's concerns more directly and effectively into the development process, and to achieve an improvement in women's status in our rapidly changing world.

The Group was established in 1980 to organize the production and distribution of UN-NGO development education materials. It was the first time that United Nations agencies and non-governmental organizations had collaborated in this way, and the Group remains a unique example of co-operation between international and non-governmental institutions. Membership of the Group is open to all interested organizations.

SERIES TITLES – in order of scheduled publication

- **WOMEN AND THE WORLD ECONOMIC CRISIS** PREPARED BY JEANNE VICKERS

- **WOMEN AND DISABILITY** PREPARED BY ESTHER R. BOYLAN

- **WOMEN AND HEALTH** PREPARED BY PATRICIA SMYKE

- **WOMEN AND THE ENVIRONMENT** PREPARED BY ANNABEL RODDA

- **REFUGEE WOMEN** PREPARED BY SUSAN FORBES MARTIN

- **WOMEN AND LITERACY** PREPARED BY MARCELA BALLARA

- **WOMEN AND HUMAN RIGHTS** PREPARED BY KATARINA TOMAŠEVSKI

- **WOMEN AND THE FAMILY** PREPARED BY HELEN O'CONNELL

- **WOMEN AT WORK** PREPARED BY SUSAN BULLOCK

- **WOMEN, PARTICIPATION AND DECISION-MAKING**
  PREPARED BY MARILEE KARL

For full details, as well as order forms, please write to:
ZED BOOKS LTD, 7 CYNTHIA STREET, LONDON N1 9JF, U.K. and 165 First Avenue, Atlantic Highlands, New Jersey 07716, U.S.A.

WOMEN AND THE FAMILY

PREPARED BY HELEN O'CONNELL

Zed Books Ltd · London & New Jersey

Women and the Family was first published by Zed Books Ltd,
7 Cynthia Street, London N1 9JF, United Kingdom and 165 First Avenue,
Atlantic Highlands, New Jersey 07716, United States of America, in 1994

The views in this publication do not necessarily reflect the views of the
United Nations

Cover and book design by Lee Robinson
Cover photo: Jenny Matthews
Typeset by EMS Photosetters, Thorpe Bay, Essex
Printed and bound in the United Kingdom at The Bath Press, Avon

British Library Cataloguing in Publication Data

A catalogue record for this book is available from the British Library

ISBN 1 85649 105 6 Hb
ISBN 1 85649 106 4 Pb

Library of Congress Cataloging-in-Publication Data

A catalog record for this book is available from the US Library of Congress

CONTENTS

ACKNOWLEDGEMENTS

This book has been prepared by Helen O'Connell, writer and campaigner on women and development issues, on behalf of the **UN-NGO Group on Women and Development**, and made possible through financial contributions from the following:

- International Labour Office (ILO)
- United Nations High Commission for Refugees (UNHCR)
- United Nations Centre for Social Development and Humanitarian Affairs/ International Year of the Family Voluntary Fund (CSDHA/IYF)
- United Nations Children's Fund (UNICEF)
- United Nations Development Fund for Women (UNIFEM)
- World Food Programme (WFP)
- Royal Norwegian Ministry of Foreign Affairs

The contents of this book have been approved by the **UN-NGO Group on Women and Development**. The following organizations have made a special contribution through their participation in the editorial panel for this publication:

- International Labour Office (ILO)
- United Nations Children's Fund (UNICEF)
- United Nations Development Programme (UNDP)
- United Nations Economic Commission for Europe (ECE)
- United Nations High Commission for Refugees (UNHCR)
- United Nations Population Fund (UNFPA)
- World Food Programme (WFP)
- World Health Organization (WHO)
- American Association of Retired Persons
- Inter-African Committee on Traditional Practices Affecting the Health of Women and Children
- International Council of Women
- International Council on Social Welfare
- International Federation of Social Workers
- International Federation of Unviersity Women
- International Organization of Consumer Unions
- Isis-WICCE
- La Leche League International
- Medical Women's International Association
- Women's International League For Peace and Freedom
- World Council of Churches
- World University Services

The book has been compiled from a variety of sources so as to provide an overview and a range of views on the issues. Over seventy organizations worldwide contributed materials. Studies have been included from the following individuals and organizations: Alice Armstrong; Women and Law in Southern Africa Project; Elizabeth Clements; Leith Dunn; Chitra Ghosh; Wendy Harcourt; Korean Women's Development Institute; Rosemarie A. Mallett; Angela Mpofu; Trish Silken; Marilyn Thomson.

Overall coordination and management of the UN-NGO Group on Women and Development is provided by the United Nations Non-Governmental Liaison Service (NGLS), an inter-agency unit which fosters dialogue and cooperation between the United Nations system and the NGO community on development policy issues and North–South relations.

PREFACE

PERHAPS THE MOST fundamental challenge for social policy and practice regarding families today is to provide direction for the evolution of the concept of the family in conformity with basic human rights and social principles, and to accelerate the elimination of practices within and on account of families that are not compatible with those standards. In this process, among a multitude of interrelated issues, women and the family is a topic which should be, and is, at the forefront.

As the world's oldest form of expression of human relationship, the family has survived for thousands of years, adapting itself constantly to changing socio-economic conditions and the progress of humanity. It is universally accepted as the basic unit of society and appreciated for the important socio-economic functions that it performs. Yet, there is no simple view of the family, nor can there be a universally applicable definition. The diversity and divergence in families is a faithful reflection of the cultural pluralism of the individuals that constitute societies.

The family is a living, evolving institution, affected by socio-economic factors as well as by changes that shape the social environment in which it functions. Consequently, families are undergoing constant change, due to numerous factors, including the quest for equality between men and women and widening opportunities for women as well as shifts in values, particularly those supporting individualism. Modernization has often called into question earlier forms of family organization, and new family types have been emerging, such as the single-parent family, which do not fit the traditional characterizations of family structures such as 'nuclear' and 'extended'. Social roles are being redefined and we have been witnessing the reorganization of family forms. All these changes in

social life and in the roles ascribed to men and women have brought with them fundamental transformation of lifestyles and personal aspirations. The increased prevalence of single-parent families, most of which are headed by women, poses important challenges for legal, social and governmental policy-makers.

Changes and transformations have brought both gains and losses. The challenge today is to reinforce positive changes and anchor them in the new social contract that is being evolved, and, at the same time, to remedy the negative consequences of change, without dampening the momentum for positive evolution. The International Year of the Family, proclaimed for 1994 by the General Assembly of the United Nations, may be viewed as an attempt at this task.

Because of the intimate nature of family relationships, negative behaviour or exploitation may be tolerated within families. Social policy should seek to educate and inform family behaviour to eliminate anti-social or detrimental practices. It should foster equality between women and men, including equality in their roles as spouses and parents; it should encourage a more equitable distribution of family resources and a more flexible sharing of household and parental responsibilities in order to create greater opportunities for women within and outside the family. An important goal should indeed be the implementation, as they apply to women and the family, of the Nairobi Forward-looking Strategies for the Advancement of Women and the United Nations Convention on the Elimination of All Forms of Discrimination against Women.

Women and the Family is a significant contribution toward meeting the challenge. Dialogue and information exchange are vital, and development education is crucial, in policy formulation and implementation. The Women and Development series of the UN-NGO Group on Women and Development has been a valuable input to the process. *Women and the Family* is an extremely timely contribution to the series, which successfully tackles various aspects of this complex topic. Undoubtedly, it is a valuable tool to foster further action toward evolving new social contracts that advance the cause of all individuals of society on the basis of equality and fundamental freedoms.

HENRYK J. SOKALSKI
Coordinator for the International Year of the Family

INTRODUCTION

WOMEN ARE SEEN as inseparable from the family, and most functions assigned to the family are allocated to women within it. Women are usually the carers, the nurturers, the educators, the source of stability, and increasingly they are major cash contributors. For the most part, women meet their responsibilities to their children, their men and older or infirm relatives with generosity, self-sacrifice and unstinting labour. Many men similarly are devoted to the creation and maintenance of the family and demonstrate respect for its individual members.

A correct understanding of the remote past can help us see ahead and move forward more surely.[1]

In the span of human history, 'civilized' society as we know it has occupied a very short time. Anthropologists who have investigated the early stages of human development identified three great epochs of social evolution: a time of hunting and gathering which lasted over 1 million years; followed by around 5,000 years during which food production, agriculture and stock raising were developed; and then a period of commodity production and exchange which has lasted to date around 3,000 years.

Investigators of early society found a social structure quite different from ours: they found a clan and tribal system, based on maternal kinship, in which women played a leading role; they found egalitarian social and sexual relations arising from collective production and communal possession of property. The father-family and male supremacy, private property and class divisions are relatively recent constructions.

The family affects every aspect of women's lives: their socialization and education, their sexuality, the way in which they are expected to behave as women, wives, mothers, and carers. The family places immense obligations on women's shoulders and shapes their place and rewards in the labour market, their role in the community and in local, national and international affairs. The location of women primarily within the private world of the family has profound implications. Respect for the family's privacy, though always selective, guides governments' largely hands-off attitudes to the division of labour, to the distribution of income within families and to male violence against women. In turn, acceptance of the division of family-related labour between women and men shapes governments' policies in all areas, such as education, employment, child care, health care and social security.

Many families now live in situations of considerable hardship, and family life is experiencing great change: rising unemployment and poverty due to economic and environmental problems make family life difficult for many. There are now over 20 million refugees in the world and around another 25 million people displaced within their own countries. Traditional family structures are changing due to economic developments and migration to urban areas. The divorce rate is high in many countries, the number of single-parent families is rising and many children live apart from their fathers and some from their mothers. There is considerable instability in relations between women and men in many countries as some of the advantages that accrued to women from family life, such as status and some financial security or protection, are no longer secure or have lost their value. The asymmetry between the family rights and responsibilities of women and of men is now more clearly understood and this knowledge is leading many women not to deny the family, but to challenge its structures. In some societies the line between women's and men's roles has become blurred as men assume greater caring responsibilities; in other cases this line has become more pronounced as many men cannot or do not contribute emotional support, labour or finance to the family.

The family, in one form or another, is the basic unit of all societies. It exists not only objectively as the recognized basic social unit but subjectively in the minds and imagination of all peoples and individuals.[2] It is widely regarded as a useful and a positive institution essential for the emotional care and development of children. The family is praised by all major world religions and most governments. The Preamble of the Convention on the Rights of the Child (1989) states that:

... the family, as the fundamental group of society and the natural environment for the growth and well-being of all its members and particularly children, should be afforded the necessary protection and assistance so that it can fully assume its responsibilities within the community.

We are all members of families, and most of us form relationships, have children and make new families. Important events in our lives take place in the family: birth, marriage, death. Each family is unique but shares characteristics with others.

The family has contradictions. It can be a shelter, offering its members security and protection from the hardships of the outside world and a place of nurturing and personality-building – 'the centre for culture, learning, and especially, economic and affective solidarity'; simultaneously, it can be restrictive and a hindrance to emotional development 'in certain cases destroying individuality and often severely sanctioning divergences'.[3] The family's paradoxical nature attracts much criticism and is regarded by some as an inherent flaw. Critics are inspired by the

concerns of politics, psychological and social interests, and feminist analysis. Writers with leftist political views have a tendency to see the family as the bastion of conservatism. Engels criticized the monogamous bourgeois family with its accompanying male domination of women. The three-generational family system in Japan was censured after the Second World War as the notion that had supported militarism and had harmed the development of democratic institutions.[4]

Those concerned about individuals' psychological and emotional well-being are critical of the family's record. They argue that it can be a detrimental influence and environment which nurtures or socializes children only in restrictive and distorted ways.[5] Many women writers too have drawn attention to the hierarchical and patriarchal structure of most family types, the arena of women's subordination and the architecture of discriminatory gender roles. The feminist appraisal opened for public view the privacy of family life and exposed not only affection and protection but also inequality and misogyny. It refuted the view that the gender division of roles within the family was natural and ordained. Mitchell writes:

... women are offered a universe of their own: the family. Like woman herself, the family appears as a natural object, but it is actually a cultural creation. There is nothing inevitable about the form or role of the family, any more than there is about the character or role of women.[6]

Questions abound in the literature on the family, whilst answers are few. Does economic development inevitably promote the appearance of the nuclear family? Will all families be standardized in the context of the general process of deculturization resulting from mass media?[7] Why cannot the family prevent such problems as alcoholism, drug abuse, suicides and mental disorders?[8] Is the family a retreat from society, a place where socialization takes place in the interests of capitalism, a convenient place to keep surplus female labour, or an affective unit?[9]

RENEWED INTEREST □ The family is on the international agenda. A number of international conferences have already taken place and in 1988, UNESCO started a process of reflection on the future of the family. The United Nations has dedicated the year 1994 to the family under the theme of: 'Family: resources and responsibilities in a changing world'. It aims to build greater awareness of the family as the natural, fundamental unit of society.

There is strong feeling that the needs of the

International Year of the Family — 1994

Principles:

- The family constitutes the basic unit of society and therefore warrants special attention;

- Families assume diverse forms and functions from one country to another, and within each national society. These express the diversity of individual preferences and societal conditions;

- Activities for IYF will seek to promote the basic human rights and fundamental freedoms accorded to all individuals by the set of internationally agreed instruments formulated under the aegis of the United Nations, whatever the status of each individual and whatever the form and condition of that family;

- Policies will aim at fostering equality between women and men within the family and to bring about a fuller sharing of domestic responsibilities and employment opportunities;

- Activities for the IYF will be undertaken at all levels – local, national, regional and international;

- Programmes should support families in the discharge of their functions, rather than provide substitutes for such families. They should promote

the inherent strengths of families, including their great capacity for self-reliance, and stimulate self-sustaining activities on their behalf;

- The IYF will constitute an event within a continuing process.

The United Nations expressed confidence that the year would offer a unique opportunity for mobilizing efforts, particularly at the local and national levels to:

- highlight the importance of families;

- promote a better understanding of the family's functions and problems;

- strengthen national institutions to formulate, implement and monitor policies in respect of the family.

Source: UN, *1994 International Year of the family: building the smallest democracy at the heart of society*, Vienna, 1991.

family as a unit have been neglected and its importance has been ignored in attempts to provide for its individual members: children, youth, the elderly, women and men. The rapid changes which have taken place recently in family formation, for example, the rise in single-parent families, are the subject of much research and discussion. Some regard these changes as a sign that the family no longer performs well, or that the social and economic situation in many countries makes it impossible for the family to fulfil its role effectively. In either case, it is argued that the family needs urgent attention. Some writers believe that in troubled times we turn to the family for stability and reassurance. Others are more sceptical and regard renewed interest in the family as more to do with a desire to limit the state's social role than with any genuine commitment to family life. It would be incorrect to attribute all renewed interest to pragmatism alone.

In certain situations, this renewed focus on the family probably contains within it, consciously or unconsciously, a reappraisal of women's gradual achievement of social, economic and political rights. There is a tendency to lay the blame for many of the new trends, such as divorce, and such social ills as drugs or vandalism, at the door of women's growing independence and therefore to want to limit or reverse that independence. Such a move would be entirely reprehensible. Women's equality and the removal of gender constraints are the essential foundation stones of juster societies in which families can thrive.

In the context of renewed interest in the family unit, it is important not to lose sight of women and thus the idea for this book was born. We want to provide an overview of what is happening to the family worldwide and to women's roles within it and to explore the relationship between the family and women's social, economic and political rights. Clearly, it is impossible to do justice

to each family situation as the cultural climate and sensitivities are so different from one community to the next. This book draws on existing research, the published materials and documents of international agencies and non-governmental organizations (NGOs) and is intended as an introduction to some of the many issues surrounding the family. Almost no issue is irrelevant, but not all could be addressed. The book is set in the context of changes which dominate our times: new social attitudes and behaviour, the technological revolution, the debt crisis, structural adjustment programmes, military conflicts and the environmental crisis – all of which have a profound impact on the family and women's roles within it.

Throughout the book the term 'family' is used in the sense of any domestic grouping but also in an extended sense to include grandparents, siblings and other relatives. The term 'marriage' is used to include civil, religious or customary marriages and common-law, consensual, living-together or living-apart unions. Likewise the terms 'wife', 'husband', 'partner' are used loosely. For convenience, 'South' is used to cover the countries of Africa, Latin America, the Caribbean, Asia with the exception of Japan, and parts of the Pacific and the Middle East; and 'North' to cover the industrialized countries. All such global terms are unsatisfactory as they hide the range of gender, class, racial and religious differences within each community, country and region.

Chapter 1 looks at some of the main patterns of family formation and structure and the changes that have taken place in the second half of the twentieth century. Chapters 2, 3 and 4 survey women's multiple and changing roles within the family. Chapter 5 looks at the status of the girl child and women within the family, and at violence. Chapter 6 focuses on the influence of religion and culture, the economic and environmental situation, and the problems caused by war, military oppression and exile. Chapter 7 charts some attempts to eliminate discrimination and looks at the role of the state both in fostering equality and in supporting families. The final chapter offers some general conclusions. Throughout the book examples are given of action that women are taking – in their communities, workplaces, nationally and internationally – to improve the situation of themselves, their families and their communities.

1. E. Reed, *Women's Evolution: from matriarchal clan to patriarchal family*, New York, Pathfinder Press, 1975.

2. UNICEF, *Introduction to Some Guiding Principles on the Family*, 1989.

3. J. Prieur, Introductory Report to the UNESCO International Conference on Families and Cultures, 4–5 December 1987, Paris.

4. K. Morioka, 'Demographic family changes in contemporary Japan', *International Social Science Journal*, No. 126, November 1990, pp. 511–22.

5. R. D. Laing and A. Esterson, *Sanity, Madness and the Family*, London, Penguin, 1964.

6. J. Mitchell, 'Women: the longest revolution,' in N. Glazer-Malbin and H. Youngelson Waehrer, *Women in a Man-made World*, Chicago, Rand McNally and Co., 1975.

7. Prieur.

8. P. Somlai, 'Families and culture in Eastern Europe', paper presented to the UNESCO International Conference on Families and Cultures, Paris, 4–5 December 1989.

9. L. J. Jordanova, 'The history of the family', in Cambridge Women's Studies Group (eds.), *Women in Society*, London, Virago, 1981, pp. 41–51.

FAMILY
OR FAMILIES?

Any model of the main characteristics of the family at the end of the twentieth century must strive to reproduce the dynamic character of the phenomenon: it has to put emphasis on the changes in the family, both as an institution of society and as a framework of individual life.[1]

INDIVIDUALS RELATED BY KIN, children, blood relatives and in-laws are normally regarded as family members. All societies and cultures have groupings, mostly founded in kinship, which exist between the society at large and the individual and which, ideally, prepare people for life in the wider community.

While there is no universally applicable definition of the family, there is a broad consensus about the role of the family in society and the functions it should perform, namely, procreation, socialization, providing affection and emotional support. In particular the family has a central role in the education, socialization and care of children. Children need care and help during their early years and, usually, this assistance is given within a family group by a parent or parents, a relative, or, in the case of adoption, a legal guardian. The family group usually provides love, care, intimacy and protection, especially to infants and children, but also to other members, including the elderly, disabled and infirm. It begins the process of each child's socialization and lays the foundations from which relationships are built with people outside the family.[2] The family plays a central role in preserving and transmitting cultural values from one generation to the next.

Families are based on the idea of mutual solidarity and exchange of services. Each family has an elaborate system of expectation, delivery and exchange of different kinds of support. A large multi-generational family has one system of rules; a single-parent family has a different set of understandings. The kinds of mutual assistance vary widely. Finch[3] identified five main kinds of support relatives provide for each other: economic, accommodation, personal care, practical help and child care, and emotional and moral support. Parents are expected to, and for the most part do, provide a full range of support to young children and teenagers: a home, food to eat, health care, other physical necessities and emotional, moral and social support. Although many family relationships are characterized by tension, family members usually make great efforts to care for, love, respect and protect each other; this is especially noticeable when one family member is in trouble or when the family unit is attacked from outside.[4]

Obey kinship rules

The ultimate aim of Dakota life, stripped of accessories, was quite simple: one must obey kinship rules; one must be a good relative. In the last analysis every other consideration was secondary... Without that aim and the constant struggle to attain it, the people would no longer be Dakotas in truth. They would no longer even be human. To be a good Dakota, then, was to be humanized, civilized. And to be civilized was to keep the rules imposed by kinship for achieving civility, good manners, and a sense of responsibility towards each individual dealt with.

Ella Cara Deloria,
a Dakota Native American, 1944[5]

Families all around the world like to gather around the dinner table: a family in a viilage near Iloilo City, the Philippines.

FAMILY TYPES AND PATTERNS □ The words most accurately used about patterns of family formation and structure as we know them in modern times are 'complexity' and 'diversity'. Almost everything one writes about family types is a generalization. Throughout any one person's life, she or he can live in a number of different family types and each is evolving continually. Families range from the large extended, through the nuclear, to the single-parent. Some families are patrilineal and patrilocal, others matrilineal and matrilocal, or combinations of either. Most are patriarchal but the familial power of the 'patriarch' varies widely from one culture to another.

The study of family typology has gained new importance in recent decades and has become the focus of much research and writing. The conventional method of identifying family types, that is by household composition, is regarded as no longer appropriate when obvious family members, such as fathers, mothers or young adults, may reside apart as migrant workers or students. A criterion other than co-residence has to be taken into account. In 1989, Louis Roussel[6] wrote of five family types: the traditional, the modern, the association-like, the club-like and one which is based on the recognition that change in the marital relationship is inevitable. Following on from this, Cseh-Szombathy[7] defined eight family types based on attitudinal and behavioural differences which in his view are the most appropriate when defining families in the late twentieth century. His categories are: traditional, modern stable, modern broken, serial marriage (remarried couple), open marriage, unmarried cohabitation, living-apart-together arrangement and inner-directed, rational marriage. This variety in family forms has led many writers to argue that it is more accurate to speak of 'families' than it is to speak of 'the family'. For the purposes of this section, it is convenient to take some broad categories, with the expectation that the complexity of the human reality will be conveyed through the later chapters.

2

THE EXTENDED FAMILY The extended family run by a (male) elder with his wife or wives and his sons' households under his authority is the traditional and dominant family unit in many countries, for example, most countries in west Africa. In the extended family, a wife is under the authority not only of the family head but also of her mother-in-law and has to obey the orders of older sisters-in-law too. In matrilineal societies, the family has a female and a male head who hold ritualistic and political responsibilities respectively.

Kin ties are much more important than conjugal in extended families and the residential household and the biological family of parents and their children are usually not identical: children may live away from their parents' home, while in a polygamous society not all wives live with their husband. Also the family goes through various stages in the cycle of births, marriages and deaths. In addition to the male head's biological family the household may include other blood relations and even more distant relatives. When several family nuclei share a compound under the same head it is difficult to say where one residential unit stops and others start.[8]

The rules governing the ownership of property and inheritance vary. For example, in sub-Saharan Africa, some societies are patrilineal, others matrilineal. Women and men rarely own property in common. In matrilineal societies, women and men may each own property jointly with other matrilineal kin.

THE THREE-GENERATION FAMILY Three-generation family units are common in many cultures. The 'stem' family, the traditional unit in Japan, is a particularly interesting example. Its primary aim is to maintain its members' way of life, family possessions and occupations, and status in the community. As a rule, one married son, usually the eldest, of the household head is regarded as the successor to the headship and heir to the family property. He remains in the parental home, forming a single household. As in the extended family, family lineage is more important than marriage: great emphasis is placed on the relation between self and parents and ancestors but not between self and spouse. The purpose of marriage is to obtain heirs for the house, so in the event of a childless marriage the daughter-in-law must be returned to her family, or an heir adopted. Safeguarding the continuity of the family is of primary importance.[9]

The stem family includes not only living members but also ancestors and descendants and sometimes persons not directly related by kinship. The hierarchy of the position of each member is well developed. Family property is held by the family head as an individual and not by the family as a collective entity. If a family head proves irresponsible, he can be replaced by a more reliable member; management skills often take precedence over kinship.

The 'joint family' in India, which is the major system even allowing for regional and cultural differences, also comprises three generations sharing one household. The father as the head of the family owns the property and as he grows older becomes the trustee of the family property and fortunes for other adult males. Traditionally, a woman is regarded as part of the property, initially of her father, then of her husband and after his death, of her sons. The joint family system is typical of upper-caste and property-owning families. Tribal communities and the caste groups who cannot own property usually live in nuclear-type families.[10]

THE NUCLEAR FAMILY Europe and North America are regarded as the home of the nuclear family, but in reality there, like elsewhere, there are many diverse cultures and an infinite variety of family types. There are differences between black and white communities, and also ethnic, language and religious variations. The nuclear family typically is a unit of parents and children. Its advent is still the subject of debate: some argue that it has been in existence for many centuries; others see it as a direct product of the Industrial Revolution. In the concept of the traditional nuclear family, the man is seen as the breadwinner and head of the family with the woman as full-time mother and housewife. Women are regarded as the intermediary between the social state and the daily life of individuals. In practice, this model was, and is, typical only of some middle- and high-income families. The concept has now evolved to take into account the many nuclear families where both partners are in paid employment. While the smaller domestic unit and the conjugal couple are long-established facts, larger family units including three generations or more are still to be found.

NEW FAMILY FORMS One-parent families – mothers, in around 90 per cent of cases – have always existed as a result of separation, desertion or widowhood. Children born outside marriage and cared for by women on their own are also not a new phenomenon However, in the past three to four decades, migration, rising divorce rates and changing social attitudes, in addition to separation and widowhood, have all contributed to a rapid increase in the number of one-parent families. Studies from southern Africa show that as many as 40 to 60 per cent of spouses are separated at any one time. This is causing concern in many societies especially as households maintained by women are disproportionately ranked among the poorest income groups in all societies (see Chapter 4).

Non-traditional types of nuclear family are growing number as more and more couples are cohabiting or forming consensual unions. Some marry at a later stage but many remain in consensual unions long-term. This trend applies particularly in Latin America, Europe and North America. In France 30 per cent of cohabiting couples in 1989 had already been together for more than five years.[11] In Quebec in 1985, the parents of 35 per cent of first-born children were unmarried.

There are also a few families, mainly in the North, composed of homosexual adults with children. Greater, but limited, tolerance has enabled homosexuality to become more open. While in some places homosexual marriages have legal standing they still face difficulties; in Denmark, for example, a homosexual married couple cannot adopt a child.

COMMON THREADS Although there is great variety in the shape, size, behavioural patterns and attitudes of families from one society to another, there are some striking cross-cultural similarities. Prieur identified some: three generations living together, 'the ambivalent role of women who are both mistress of the home and subject to the domination of the men', parental authority over their children, and the role of rituals and ceremonies.[12]

Women's position within different family types varies enormously. Rights to own property, access to education, civil and social status all shape this position, as do the nature of the family hierarchy, the extent of women's autonomy, and levels of class and racial privilege. In some societies, the family is attempting to devise more egalitarian structures, while others are characterized by segregation between women and men. Many women are gaining greater personal autonomy and social and economic independence, while others are experiencing sexual, economic and political subjugation.

As with the family, generalizations about women need continuous qualification. However, it is true to say that hierarchical gender relations are widespread and that, universally, women have primary responsibility for rearing children, caring for other adults and running the household.

WOMEN AND THE FAMILY IN THE CARIBBEAN*
Rosemary Mallett

The Caribbean has always presented a very dynamic arena in which to analyse gender (social) relations because of the culturally specific form which mating patterns, family formation and gendered identities have taken. There is general agreement that illegitimacy rates are high, marriage rates are low, and that women play a prominent role in the domestic and kinship domains.

PATRIARCHY AND THE FAMILY STRUCTURE

Patterns of family formation in the Caribbean stem in part from the cultural patterns of the slave plantation – with the amalgamation of African and European value patterns and their manifestation in plantation life, and in part from the socio-economic developments of the post-slavery period. Almost one-third of the households are in fact *de jure* female-headed, and up to another one-sixth are female-maintained or supported by a woman.

Many of the earlier researchers on the family in the Caribbean equated social organization with domestic organization, and firmly centred women at the core of family structures and men outside. This led to the myth of the Afro-Caribbean family being viewed as matriarchal and the society as matrifocal.

Female headship has always been high in the region since slavery, due to factors such as greater female longevity, mating practices during slavery, and after emancipation extensive male migration out of the smaller islands. Caribbean women have always worked, Afro-Caribbean women working alongside men on the plantations during and after slavery. However, to deduce from

these historically high levels of economic independence and female household headship that the Caribbean is a matrifocal society is to conflate economic autonomy with social power and to assume that one leads to the other. Such analyses ignored the interrelationship of factors which resulted in these Caribbean households being organized in differing fashions and in the sexual division of labour in the private and public domains.

Almost all of the early studies viewed the Eurocentric image of the male authoritarian breadwinner as normative, and presumed from the high level of male absence from households that men lacked authority in, and were marginal to the household and family.

From such a characterization of the Caribbean household one might be led to suppose that the household became a base of women's power and autonomy and that the family was therefore not necessarily the main site of women's oppression. However, while regarded as a powerful socializing agency and major institution in society, in effect the family is also deemed to be subsumed under or encompassed within the wider social operations of the public domain which men control. Women's horizons are expected to be limited to a small range of closely related kin and their immediate needs, and women are subordinated by a traditional patriarchal structuring of gender roles and responsibilities. While patriarchy is thus not specifically premissed upon male headship of the household, the fact that many women and men continue to aspire to the 'normative' or ideal model of male headship in all spheres may mean that patriarchy may be based on a normative/ideal if unrealistic definition of the family.

* Rosemary Mallett is a former Research Fellow at the Institute of Social and Economic Research, University of the West Indies, Cave Hill. She is presently a Research Officer at the Medical Research Council, London.

5

THE CONTEMPORARY SITUATION

The accession of Caribbean people to independent government, to universal primary and secondary education, and concomitantly to better-paying and more professional occupations has enabled men and women of Afro-Caribbean descent to transcend class barriers. These socio-economic developments have, like elsewhere in the world, transformed the way women operate within society and in the family.

Over the last thirty years traditional mobility patterns have been assailed and women have entered senior management and administrative positions in both the private and public sectors. In some countries the proportion of women in white-collar work, particularly in the civil service and teaching, in some instances clearly outstrips male participation.

This has led in recent years to a male counter-reaction to the increasing visibility of women in the public sphere and to a questioning of the role of women in society. Some male academics are now raising concerns over the lack of male role models in schools for boys and the tremendous success in girls' secondary-school achievements, which some feel may result in female preponderance in prominent positions and, to a certain extent, male marginality.

CONCLUSION

When studying gender relations one also needs to look at the basis and distribution of power and influence between the genders in households and in the wider society. There is a need to focus upon the link between the social construction of gender, that is, the acquisition of gender identity, and the political economy of gender. The system of gender relations includes sexual relations between adults in and outside households, the relations between households, the sexual division of labour both in and outside the household, and the socialization of gender roles.

A theory of gender for the Caribbean must focus upon the interaction of social change and culture, and the impact of social and economic changes upon gender identity formation, in order to try to come to some understanding of the diverse ways in which women and men are bound together in social units that cross-cut gender divisions.[13] ●

CHANGES IN THE FAMILY ☐ Despite massive research, historians have failed to locate 'a golden age of the family'.[14] Rather, the evidence indicates that flux and inequalities characterize the family throughout its history.

In modern times, including the last 3,000 years, some type of unit resembling a family has existed and has shown both resistance and flexibility to change. Throughout, many of the family's functions remained intact. Family patterns have been affected by colonization, slavery, cultural and ideological influences and political circumstances, but perhaps most fundamentally by the development of modern capitalism: growing industrialization and urbanization have separated home from paid employment and family members from each other. The twentieth century has exposed the family to unprecedented pressure: political, scientific and technological revolutions, economic and environmental crises, ideological confusion and military strife. A number of other specific factors have had considerable influence on the family: improvements in transport and communications have given most people access to information about lifestyles, values and behavioural norms different to those of their own societies; increased access to education and formal-sector employment, especially for women, has brought new attitudes; and generalized access to methods of regulating fertility has altered sexual relations.

The extent of the changes varies widely within communities, countries and regions, but it is possible to identify some common trends: the weakening of some traditional family ties and the emergence of new forms of family solidarity; changing relations between women and men within the family, and rising divorce rates; fewer children per family, and increasing longevity.

THE WEAKENING OF TRADITIONAL FAMILY TIES
Migration from rural to urban areas, and the consequent growth of large cities, have had dramatic and instant effects on traditional family life. Over the past three decades or more, women and men from Southern countries have migrated to escape rural poverty and seek new employment. In general, more men that women migrate but in recent years the number of women has increased. Latin America is the exception: young women under fifteen are the majority of migrants. Large numbers of women from the Philippines and elsewhere seek work abroad.

Migration affects many aspects of family life. The strong family ties that thrive when family members live in close proximity and which offer great support and stability to family life can be weakened by the separation of family members. Migration can result in more freedom for young women and men living away from the watchful eyes, the expectations and the values of parents, relatives and close community, but can also bring new problems. The traditional authority of older family members over younger is diminished. Sexual life is one area in which the erosion of social control is most noticeable. In some African countries, as young men with access to cash income no longer need rely on their fathers and relatives to pay brideprice for them, the authority of the father and the strong family ties are lessened.[15]

The move to a town or city is accompanied by new ways of living: usually home and paid work are separated, whilst family childcare assistance and emergency support may no longer be readily available. It has been recorded that when women and men live in towns away from the collective control of the family, the durability of their marriages or unions is weakened. People have no one to whom they can turn for support when problems arise within the marriage. Many men who migrate from rural areas leave women, children and older relatives behind to cope with added responsibilities and workloads. When men have jobs in the modern sector, women have no access to their income or little means of bringing pressure to bear on them to contribute towards family needs.[16]

In Japan, *tanshin hunin*, job transfers of mid-life and middle-income men who are not accompanied by family members, are now widespread. Frequent movement of children from one locality to another is considered detrimental to their education, so fathers move alone and visit their families at weekends. The incidence of alcoholism and depression is increasing among such separated men, whilst women become, in effect, single parents. The sharing of food among all family members, once a sacred ritual and the most basic function of the family, is no longer possible. The results from one survey indicate that about 60 per cent of fathers were missing at the breakfast table, and about 30 per cent at the dinner table.[17]

THE CONCEPT OF THE FAMILY IN INDIAN SOCIETY[*]
Chitra Ghosh

The family in India has been accepted as a holistic institution in the true sense. The genealogy passes from father to son, the belief in Hindu scriptures being that the

* Chitra Ghosh, of the International Federation of University Women, is a Fellow in the Department of Social and Political History of South and South East Asian Studies at the Netaji Institute of Asian Studies, Calcutta.

Three generations often live under the same roof, like this Nicaraguan family.

dead soul gains deliverance after receiving obeisance from the hands of the succeeding generations of male heirs. It is not only in religious matters but in economic succession as well that primogeniture is the rule. The family being the unit of production, what one receives is generally determined according to one's needs, though everyone is expected to put in her or his best efforts. The society is basically monolithic and masculine, except for certain tribal areas where a matriarchal social system prevails.

During the decades since independence and in consequence of the reformulation of the legal system, Indian society has undergone considerable economic and socio-demographic transformation. With accelerated urbanization and the expansion of industrialization, coupled with increased rural-urban migration, the end of the monopoly of land occupancy by the few rich and the spread of education, a significant

social change has taken place. The existing norms and values, primarily based on religious sanctions, have eroded. The centrality of the perennial household as an entity still exists, but different notions and principles guide it.

The question is: how far is the family still the centre for gender subordination? The role differentiation between men and women is determined by caste, religion and cultural norms, and influences to a large extent their work and mobility. Today financial power, which is generally wielded by the menfolk, has been added to the list. Consequently, male children predominate; mothers are still guided by the 'risk factor' of losing them, and sons are regarded as an 'honour factor' when young and as subsistence when the parents become old and infirm. Much concern therefore is being shown at the disappearance of the joint family system. As the boys are looked upon as patrilineal permanent members and the girls as transient members of the family structure, the latter are regarded as expendable. The dowry system is an outcome of this mentality: take as much in dowry as possible.

The early age of marriage for girls also developed from these changes as well as from their seclusion and the non-inclination of parents to spend money on their girl children or to send them to school. Education may give girls opinions, ideas, which may not be to the liking of their elders. The invisible *purdah* (curtain) dominates the girl's life and activities – what she can see, with whom she can interact, where she can go – in general what she does with her life. The veiling, or the *ghunghat*, has gone but the strain remains. It predetermines the status of the woman in the Indian family. Son preference is as strong as ever: it even determines the pattern of allocation of household resources. So whilst sex roles are based on physical distinction, gender difference is social and cultural.

The domestication of women is thus linked in terms of housework and child care, which continues to hold the balance in the adjustment of family relationships. ●

WOMEN-MEN RELATIONS Many women no longer acquiesce to the old system of values governing the traditional assignment of roles within the family. Changes in women's legal status in many countries, improved access to education and new job opportunities have begun to alter the balance of power between women and men. Access to some level of economic independence has enabled many women to delay marriage or leave an unsatisfactory marriage. Divorce is increasing worldwide (see Chapter 2).

Women's attitudes to themselves, to men, to marriage and to the family are changing. In particular, many women are questioning men's power within the family. Economic changes and migration have resulted in

many women playing an even greater part than previously in providing for their children's daily subsistence, through food production in rural areas and/or through other kinds of paid work. When women bear most of the expenses of the household's daily life while men make disbursements selectively for specific expenditures, women are less likely to welcome or respect men's traditional authority. Men have changed very little and are changing more slowly; some would say that they have more to lose.

The development of modern contraceptives, such as the 'pill', and their widespread use since the mid-1970s enabled many women to decide when and if to have children, and how many. The importance to women of controlling their fertility cannot be overstated: it has opened new opportunities for women to plan their lives. Although in Africa, Asia and Latin America most women do not yet have access to safe, appropriate and inexpensive contraceptives (see Chapter 2), the generalized availability of contraception has had profound effects on relations between women and men.

Advances in biotechnology also have had new and widely unforeseen implications for sexual relations and for family matters. Although the possibility of artificial insemination confronts society with new ethical and cultural problems, related to *in vitro* fertilization and surrogacy for example, it also makes new socio-cultural behaviour possible.[18] Advances in reproductive technology have aroused heated debate among researchers: some see the technological advances as detrimental to women, as just one more medical intervention; others argue that the real issue is who controls the technology, and stress that it can be of benefit to women, for example those unable to conceive.

FAMILY SIZE AND AGE RATIOS The 'demographic transition' from high mortality and fertility to low is an important change in

9

family formation; some argue it is as far-reaching in its impact as industrialization.[19] Decades of emphasis on family planning and the virtues of the small family, combined with the availability of contraception and women's greater access to education and higher-paid jobs in the formal economy, have succeeded in reducing birth rates in most countries. Simultaneously, medical and scientific advances throughout the twentieth century have resulted in women and men living longer, with women comprising the majority of older people. China and the US both have 6 million people over 65 years of age. By the year 2005 nearly one in three elderly Americans (that is, those 65 and over) will be over 80 years old.[20] At present in Latin America and the Caribbean there are 7.5 million women and men over 60 years old, approximately 4 million of whom are women. In Africa the numbers are much lower: people over 60 years old account for only 6 per cent of the population. Sweden is the world's 'oldest' country with 17 per cent of its population being elderly whilst Japan has one of the most rapidly aging populations, whose life expectancy has increased since 1945 from 62 to 76 for men, and from 61 to 81 for women.

It should be a happy occurrence that women and men are living longer and that four- or five-generational families are becoming more common. However, it is also a cause for concern. Most older women, and many older men, live in generally poor socio-economic conditions and whilst most men die married, most women are alone in their last years. Also, the shifts in population ratios between young and old put more caring responsibilities in fewer and fewer hands.

HOUSEHOLD SIZE Fewer children does not automatically mean smaller household units. The economic situation in many countries has necessitated the strengthening of family and kin solidarity at a very practical level.

Urbanization has not led inevitably to nuclear family units; rather, there seems to be an increase in the average size of households. In Kenya, households are generally larger in urban than in rural areas.[21] Various reasons are suggested for this. The rising age of first marriage means that young adults remain in their parental family for longer, and economic difficulties hamper couples establishing separate residential units. In addition, individuals who migrate to the cities usually live with other family members and frequently depend on them for employment.[22] In Brazil, although the general trend is towards smaller households, poverty and housing shortages have contributed to an increase in the numbers of complex households, that is, units with a couple, or adult women, unmarried children and non-relatives.[23]

CONCLUSION ☐ Undeniably, the family in most societies is undergoing extraordinary and revolutionary changes, though in some areas these changes are taking place more slowly and subtly. Some, but by no means all changes in family formation and structure could be regarded as progressive. Many women and men are now able to exert more control over their own destinies and enjoy greater opportunities than before. Conversely, whereas forty years ago almost everyone was living in a family unit of one kind or another, now significant numbers of adult women and men are temporarily or permanently detached from their immediate natal and/or conjugal family through divorce, migration and exile, or choice. Since the 1960s the relations between women and men and attitudes to family matters have altered significantly; whilst this is generally for the better, we cannot forget that at the same time women's family responsibilities are increasing.

Although family members are generally more dispersed, the concept of family

Traditional family structures of Native Americans have undergone a tremendous change. A mother and son, Ohio, USA.

appears to be as important as ever to most people's lives, and family bonds are still strong and meaningful. For the most part, and despite profound changes in our societies, the family, in all its forms, continues to perform most of the social

functions expected of it. It is the location in which children, the elderly, the infirm and those with disabilities receive emotional, practical and economic support. It remains, too, the significant communicator of cultural values.

1. L. Cseh-Szombathy, 'The family at the end of the twentieth century', paper prepared for the Second Ad Hoc Inter-agency Meeting on the International Year of the Family, Vienna, 5-6 March 1992.

2. J. Moerman, 'The family today and its prospects for tomorrow', paper presented to a meeting in Budapest, 28 August 1987.

3. J. Finch, *Family Obligations and Social Change*, Cambridge, UK, Polity Press, 1989.

4. Moerman.

5. Cited in P. Gunn, *Spider Woman's Granddaughters: traditional tales and contemporary writings by Native American women*, London, Women's Press, 1989.

6. L. Roussel, *La famille incertaine*, Paris, Jacob, 1989.

7. Cseh-Szombathy.

8. C. Oppong, 'Family structure and women's reproductive and productive roles', in Anker, M. Buvinic and N. Yousseff (eds.), *Women's Roles and Population Trends in the Third World*, London, Croom Helm, 1982.

9. K. Kurimoto, 'The family in Japanese culture', paper presented to the International Conference on Families and Cultures, Paris, UNESCO, 3-4 December 1987.

10. M. Mukhopadhyay, *Silver Shackles: women and development in India*, Oxford, Oxfam, 1984, p. 10.

11. C. Safilios-Rothschild, 'Family expectations at present and in the future', in the *Report of the Fourth International Working Seminar in Salzburg on The Caring Society in a Threatened Economy*, Institute for Study in Salzburg, 1990, p. 57.

12. J. Prieur, Introductory Report to the International Conference on Families and Cultures, Paris, UNESCO, 4-5 December 1987.

13. See J. Massiah, 'Women and the Caribbean Project; an overview', *Social and Economic Studies*, Vol. 35, No. 2, 1986; E.

Miller, *The Marginalization of the Black Male: insights from the development of the teaching profession*, ISER, 1986; N. M. Forde, 'Women and the Law', Cave Hill, ISER, University of the West Indies, 1981; S. Ortner and H. Whitehead, *Sexual Meanings; the cultural construction of gender*, Cambridge, UK, Cambridge University Press, 1982, p. 8. For the purpose of this study, 'Caribbean' is used to identify the English-speaking Caribbean countries within the regional grouping CARICOM.

14. V. M. Moghadam, 'Approaching the family, gender, development and equity', paper prepared for the Second Ad Hoc Inter-agency Meeting on the International Year of the Family, Vienna, 5-6 March 1992.

15. S. Armstrong, 'Female circumcision: fighting a cruel tradition', *New Scientist*, 2 February 1991.

16. T. Lauras-Lecoh, 'Family trends and demographic transition in Africa', *International Social Science Journal*, No. 126, November 1990, pp. 475-92.

17. Kurimoto.

18. D. Behnam, 'An international inquiry into the future of the family: a UNESCO project', *International Social Science Journal*, No. 126, November 1990, pp. 547-52.

19. V. M. Moghadam, 'Women and the changing family', in *Social Change and Women in the Middle East*, Boulder, CO, Lynne Rienner, forthcoming.

20. US Bureau of the Census, *An Ageing World*, 1987, p. 10.

21. Shanyisa Khasiani, in M. J. Gibson, 'West meets East at UN conference on ageing and the family - report on conference', *Ageing International*, June 1991, pp. 33-42.

22. Lauras-Lecoh, p. 485.

23. A.M. Goldani, 'Changing Brazilian families and the consequent need for public policy', *Changing Family Patterns: International Social Science Journal*, No. 126, November 1990, pp. 523-37.

ROLES
AND RIGHTS

Before it was a silent life between men and women. They never spoke to one another, not even husband and wife. Neighbouring women would pass the evenings chatting and spinning, and you would talk to other women at the wells and at the grinding stone. Women never spoke in the presence of men: they'd be ashamed and above all scared that they'd be beaten by their husbands on returning home. So women kept their ideas to themselves, even if these would have been a help to the community. Women were never allowed to inherit the land of their husband. As this is normal here, women never complain, thinking 'that's how things are'. Nowadays, the radio is a major source of information. This keeps women up to date with all the news from the area, the town, neighbouring countries and overseas.

We now have women who preside over meetings in the villages, in the local area and even in the towns. They have all been democratically elected by village groups and through other political structures. Development projects have helped women greatly in their work, through meetings and by helping them to visit different areas and exchange ideas about different social structures.

**FATIMATA SAWADOGO,
OUAHIGOUYA, BURKINA FASO[1]**

FEW DENY THAT WOMEN in every society carry out multiple roles both within the family and outside. Women have responsibilities which can be roughly categorized as: reproductive (child-bearing, -caring and -rearing); caring for other family members, the ill, the infirm and the elderly; household domestic work including food growing, buying and preparation. Side by side with these is what is called productive work: agriculture, and earning an income in the full range of trades and professions. Recently researchers have identified other areas of responsibility: community management[2] and environmental management.[3] Oppong and Abu[4] have identified seven roles: maternal occupational, conjugal, domestic, kin, community, individual. However described, and in some societies there are no terms to differentiate productive from reproductive work, it is clear that each role contains within it myriad functions and obligations that call for many different skills.

Research in various disciplines over the last thirty years has identified and described these roles and succeeded in making them visible to those who want to know. Social and economic development programmes in every country are now required, though still sometimes reluctantly, to give some recognition to the central place women hold within society. The discussion of women's multiple roles has helped focus attention on the immense demands which are made on women's time, energy, skills and good will. It also allows for a much more critical assessment of social and economic development policies and programmes, whether designed to assist national development or specifically for women. Importantly, it highlights the asymmetry in women's and men's family and public responsibilities.

The family is widely perceived as the 'natural' state for every human being and until quite recently this 'naturalness' was transferred without question to the division of roles and responsibilities within it. Young girls are socialized and trained from early childhood to take care of others, to be altruistic, loving and forgiving. Full assumption of the roles of wife, mother, carer and provider comes in most societies with marriage. This marks a woman's official, if not biological, entry to adulthood.

MARRIAGES AND UNIONS □ In modern times, in every culture, marriage is a time of celebration, feasting, music and dancing, when family and community members and friends come together and bestow gifts and blessings upon the couple. The festivity often hides a reality of poverty, family pressure, reluctant brides, unwilling grooms and discriminatory social norms.

In most societies, marriage signifies some mutual commitment by each partner. It is a public demonstration of the linking of two individuals and two families and the legitimation of reproduction. By marrying publicly the couple is seeking the endorsement, and more important, the support of family, community and friends for the union. This support is particularly critical in times of disagreement or difficulty. The absence of this 'emergency' support when migration and other factors separate the couple from their kin and community may be decisive in determining the outcome of the marriage.

There are strong social and personal reasons why women and men marry. Marriage can bring improved social status and prestige for women and men and usually some protection for women. It offers the potential for some long-term sharing of resources and shared responsibilities for children. Emotional needs for love, affection and approval, and physical desires for sexual pleasure too, are incentives to marriage. It can also be a means of forging alliances between powerful and potentially competing families: a means of amalgamating wealth, power and prestige, or of retaining property within a certain social group. Child-bearing is an essential goal of marriage in most societies. Where it is primarily an economic contract, the aim is to increase the labour power of the family through the woman's own work and that of her children.

The formality of marriage varies. Marriages can be legal, that is either civil, religious or customary; common-law, consensual unions or cohabitation; or visiting unions. Most women are married for some part of their adult life, and in most societies, South and North, women who have never married are in a small minority. The social acceptability of spinsterhood and bachelorhood is limited in many societies. Young girls in all societies are groomed for marriage from an early age. The allocation of tasks in the home and outside, the amount and kind of education received, rules of behaviour, limitations on personal freedom and constraints on sexuality are determined by the ultimate end of attracting a husband, being acceptable to his family, being the perfect wife, home-maker and future mother. Recently, in some European countries, such as Finland, the marriage rate, which had dropped significantly in the 1970s, has begun to rise again.

In a situation where women worldwide earn less than men, where the majority of women and men want children and where few alternative structures for emotional, practical or financial support exist, marriage or some other kind of union, and the hope that it will last, is the only option for many women. But marriage is not without its problems for women. As currently practised, most marriages have implicit inequalities. When women marry at a very early age, their opportunities for personal development through education, for consciousness and critical analysis of their situation can be drastically curtailed. The age of the spouse, women's lack of choice and unrealistic expectations can bring other problems.

THE MARRIAGE CONTRACT The marriage contract has been described as a contract that many women enter into without knowing its full terms or its ramifications for individual rights. With marriage women lose certain rights and gain others. In patrilocal societies women lose rights within their natal family and acquire others within their marital family. Marriage contracts, however informal and unwritten, are based on a mixture of custom and law and differ widely on such matters as the rights and duties of each spouse in relation to children, the name to be used by woman and children, the use of property and inheritance rules. Most legal systems ascribe the position of household head to the man even if he is not permanently resident. In practice, each partner's decision-making power within the marriage depends on the value of the economic assets, such as land or money, and personal abilities, such as education, each brings to the marriage and the extent of the support provided by each respective natal family.

There is a growing lobby for more formal marriage contracts, along the lines of commercial partnership contracts. These would be negotiated and agreed by each partner, as an individual and on an equal footing. Critics of this idea say that such contracts would not work, fundamentally because women and men do not have equal bargaining power.

The payment of some form of dowry by the bride's family to the groom's is common in many cultures, although its importance varies greatly from one cultural setting to another. It can be a cause of discrimination against girl children and women, as for example in India where a woman's status within marriage and in the eyes of her in-laws can be determined by the amount and quality of her dowry.[5] In some cases, the system has led to extreme violence against women, often to the point of murder (see Chapter 5). While the marriage agreement stipulates the amount of money the wife should receive from the husband in the event of divorce initiated by him, in reality the woman's ability to obtain this sum on divorce depends entirely on the power and support of her natal family.

By contrast, in some countries, for example in southern Africa, the custom is that brideprice is paid by the groom to the bride's family. Traditionally, the brideprice was land, cattle or household goods. The growing monetarization of the economies in the area has in many cases increased the demands made by the bride's family. The nature of the practice varies: in some societies the brideprice is given to the bride for her own use and is an important financial resource for her; in others it becomes the property of the bride's family to dispose of as it sees fit. If the woman later seeks a separation, the groom's family can demand the repayment of the brideprice; in situations where it is already spent or sold the bride's family is unlikely to approve of her separation or welcome her home.

AGE OF MARRIAGE The age at which women marry and/or start to bear children is tied very closely to their status within a society. Early marriage and child-bearing have serious implications for the health and well-being of the woman and her access to education and training. Overall, there is a direct link between a woman's education and the age at which she marries: the higher the level of her education, the later she will marry. Later marriage is clearly in the interests of the woman's personal development, education and well-being, as well as of the health of her children.

In some societies, unmarried women above a certain age (and that could be twelve years or younger) are quickly labelled of suspect virtue: '. . . doubts about their "purity" grow with each year they remain unmarried after this milestone has been reached'.[6] Women's sexuality and the need for men in male-dominated societies to control it are strong reasons for early marriage, a view usually endorsed by religious leaders. Furthermore, that youth and beauty are synonymous in most cultures provides yet another stimulus to early marriage.

Worldwide the average age of first marriage is rising to around twenty years for women, due mainly to a longer time spent in full-time education. This global figure hides a much lower average in some countries; in Bangladesh more than 52 per cent of girls are married before they are fifteen years old. In general, teenage marriage is more common in rural than in urban areas, which reflects the stronger adherence to tradition and the lack of opportunities for women in rural areas. In Latin America and the Caribbean, adolescent marriage is not common, but often non-legalized unions are formed in adolescence and formalized at a later age. In Northern countries the number of teenage unions is rising.

MARRIAGE IN ERITREA *

Trish Silkin

Eritrean society encompasses a number of ethno-linguistic groups which have retained many of their customary social norms and practices. Foremost among these for almost all social groups has been the practice of arranged marriage.

Abolishing arranged marriage was, from its founding in 1970, central to the social reforms initiated by the Eritrean People's Liberation Front (EPLF). The long-term aim of reform was to liberalize marriage completely, but reform campaigns came in time to focus on three more modest and achievable objectives: raising the bride's age to eighteen; reducing expenditure on weddings, dowry and bridewealth; and giving the betrothed couple the right to refuse an arranged marriage. The EPLF also, importantly, offered sanctuary to girls escaping from a forced marriage.

Two main factors determined how successful campaigns were. The first was whether villages were close to towns and already influenced by an urban, capitalist culture. It was much harder to achieve success in remote areas which had undergone very little transformation in the colonial period. The second was how well established the EPLF was. In general, the longer they had been in an area the more receptive people were to their message. By the mid-1980s almost every village had undergone a reform campaign, and most had amended their customary marriage laws in some fashion.

It was in the ranks of the EPLF that the most radical changes took place. One reason for this was the all-embracing culture of the movement, born out of shared danger and privation, and shaped by the urban intellectuals who formulated policy. Within the movement, also, the social and economic underpinnings of the arranged marriage system had disappeared, since EPLF members had almost no contact with their families, lived as members of military units even when they were married, received no salaries and owned no property. These circumstances created ideal conditions for changing attitudes and behaviour.

Free choices based on full knowledge, including sexual knowledge, of one's partner became an established norm. Contraception was available and informal unions were not expected automatically to terminate in marriage. Marriages were contracted across traditional religious and ethnic divides, and previously unthinkable arrangements were made, such as men marrying women so severely injured in combat that they required their constant care.

Not everything was swept away. Most couples did marry, and most married the only person with whom they had had a relationship. Marriages between couples of different class backgrounds were uncommon.

---

* Trish Silkin is a freelance development consultant, currently specializing in problems of food security. She is the author of a thesis documenting campaigns undertaken by the Eritrean People's Liberation Front in the 1970s and 1980s to reform marriage.

Though everyone was at least eighteen when they married, most were well into their twenties or older – both men and women still expected the wife to be somewhat younger than her husband.

In 1991, the EPLF was established as the Provisional Government of Eritrea. The new government is unlikely to undertake fresh initiatives to reform marriage as its immediate priority is to rebuild an economy which has been shattered by a thirty-year war and which has left nine-tenths of the population destitute. Moreover, the government has moved away from highly centralized efforts at social engineering towards a new policy which devolves development to communities who set their own priorities and work towards them at their own pace.

Three factors are likely to slow down the pace of change among the rural majority. The first is that they urgently need to restore their lost livelihoods. The second is the return from Sudan of almost half a million refugees who have been exposed to a more conservative culture. Finally, most people are likely to want to signal the end of the war by restoring normal community life – and this includes, importantly, celebrating marriage in its more traditional forms.●

MAIL-ORDER BRIDES The purchasing of brides from certain Asian countries, such as the Philippines or Thailand, by men from Europe, North America and Australia is a fairly recent phenomenon. It is a blatant manifestation of the inequality between women and men and of the failure to guarantee women's human rights. Through advertising and catalogues, marriage brokers and introduction bureaux offer men a choice of young brides, usually from the poorest families. After some initial correspondence and exchange of money, the prospective husband travels abroad, selects his bride, pays the fee and returns home married. Once married, a woman is in a very vulnerable position: she is usually totally dependent on her husband for legal status, income, social contacts and a home. It is no accident that young Asian women are the preferred brides; they are racially stereotyped by Northern media as docile, obedient and sexy. The mail-order bride business has been the focus of many campaigns, for example in the Philippines and the UK, which have successfully highlighted the abuses inherent in the arrangement.

HIGH EXPECTATIONS The model for marriage and consensual unions, as currently perceived by many women and men in Europe and North America, is based on an all-encompassing relationship. Women and men must share everything, a home, finance, friends and leisure time. The expectations of mutual support and solidarity are high, as well as of fidelity. The relationship must satisfy not only sexual needs but also emotional, intellectual and recreational needs, while at the same time not interfering too much with each individual's personal freedom and development. These high hopes are difficult to achieve in equal measure by each partner. The ensuing disappointment has been identified by some analysts as the motivation for separation and divorce when the commitment to personal fulfilment takes precedence over the commitment to the union.

SEXUAL RELATIONS In most societies, education for sexual relations is fragmentary, with the result that sex is surrounded with taboo, secrecy and innuendo. Women are widely regarded as sexually alluring and a potential danger to every man. It is women's sexuality, and not men's, which must be controlled and repressed, by social norms, restrictions on mobility, and violence if deemed necessary. A woman must be asexual and modest in public while always available to her husband in private. Within marriage, sexual relations are usually founded on inequality. A persistent idea is that sex is a man's right and a woman's obligation; thus men's sexual actions are legitimized and women's sexual pleasure is denied. An almost universal system of double standards exists on female and male sexuality: even in those societies where sexual relations outside marriage are explicitly forbidden, the prohibition is usually only enforced and monitored with respect to women; and where rules on sexual behaviour are assumed to be lax they are still enforced more strictly on women.

In many countries the law forbids men and women to have more than one spouse simultaneously, in others it is legal for men to have two or more wives. Polygamy as an institution continues to flourish in west Africa, in some Middle Eastern countries and in Pakistan. Lauras-Lecoh argues that even where uncommon, polygamy 'as an option is always a prospect in marital life which influences relations between spouses'.[7] In countries where polygamy as an institution is declining, it is quite common for men in certain social groups to have more than one sexual partner.

Polygamy is usually associated with a wide age gap between wives and husbands as such a gap lessens the potential tension between older and younger prospective bridegrooms. It is primarily a practice of advantage to men, both economically and demographically: in all patrilineal societies new marital unions bring additional prestige to the man since wives, through their work and children, enrich their husband's lineage.[8] Polygamy is often associated with the practice of post-partum abstinence, in which women refrain from sexual intercourse for a period of time after each child is born to avoid another pregnancy and prolong breast-feeding.

Views differ as to the advantages and disadvantages of polygamy for women. Women can benefit from being part of a group of interdependent co-wives: agricultural work can be shared and some domestic work performed in rotation, though frequently the relationship between co-wives is marked with conflict. Some have argued that educated women can also find polygamy to their advantage: they can start a family while preserving their independence.[9] Other writers strongly disagree and see polygamy as 'an oppressive practice' and one which can be explained fully only by the fact that 'polygamous men are selfish, irresponsible, thoughtless and brainwashed'. Thus, they argue, the true reason (but not justification) for polygamy is sex.[10]

The issue of inherent inequality within polygamous marriages has been raised by many writers. As polygamy is based on culturally specific attitudes to social and sexual relations, it is a difficult issue for cross-cultural discussion. Institutionalized polygamy is becoming less common, most probably due both to women's changing attitudes and to economic circumstances.

DIVORCE AND WIDOWHOOD In the USA one marriage in two ends in divorce, in the UK the proportion is one in three. Unofficial statistics for the pre-1991 USSR also put the rate of divorce at one in three. In the North as a whole, the United Nations (UN) estimates that the divorce rate tripled between 1960 and 1980 and that now between 25 and 50 per cent of marriages end in divorce. Divorce became progressively easier to obtain after the 1960s as complicated procedures were removed and public sanction diminished. In the North, women now request divorce more often than men. Indications are that the divorce rate is rising also in most Southern countries. Instability is high in marital and consensual unions in many Latin American and Caribbean countries. It is assumed that divorces and separations will increase in Africa with the rise in migration. Divorce, whether instigated by one partner or by mutual consent, is a traumatic experience for both partners but most particularly for children.

The ending of a marriage by separation, divorce or the death of the man brings specific problems for women. Many more women outlive their partners than vice versa due to men's lower life expectancy and the age differential in marriage. Broken employment records and limited pension entitlements can mean that many widows live in poverty (see chapters 4 and 7). Widowhood can be particularly harsh where customary law permits the husband's family to take over his property but does not enforce familial obligations to the widow and children. Young child widows in parts of south India are not allowed to remarry; they must return to their parents where, as burdens on the family, they can face drudgery and hostility. Legal change that recognizes women's right to inherit is one important safeguard for widows.

EQUAL IN MARRIAGE? As currently constructed in most societies, marriage is not an egalitarian institution. In some societies women and men have little say in the choice of marriage partners. Many commentators are critical of the concentration of power in men's hands which exists in many marriages and which allows men to dominate sexual, social, economic and psychological relations. Many women and men are searching for and building more egalitarian unions and marriages. Cohabitation can offer greater independence to women but is not in any way automatically synonymous with equality. Marriage without inequality is possible but unlikely to become widespread until gender inequalities within the wider society are removed.

---

*WOMEN, SEXUALITY AND THE FAMILY**
━━━━━━━━━━━━━━━ Wendy Harcourt

Sexuality and the family are crucial issues for women's rights to equal choice and freedom from fear and oppression. Women's sexual well-being, their emotional and physical security are fundamental to their social well-being and to their full participation in their country's social and economic development plans, policies and programmes.

For women, the family is the place which primarily defines their social sexual role determined by their relationship with men. Women's sexuality is linked most readily to their biological ability to reproduce. In most cultures a woman's body is seen as the primary site of sexuality, as mother and as the object desired by men. In many cultures women's own sexual desire is negated and seen as dangerous to men. Hence women are defined by their sexuality in relation to their social function as mother, wife or lover; this sexuality is not theirs, nor does it necessarily reflect their own desire or individual needs.

Almost paradoxically, women's sexuality is valued most often by their non-sexual practice (virginity) or by their fecundity and ability to bear male children, neither of which implies women's individual fulfilment. Women's sexuality is most often seen as the property of her family and valued as her marriage price.

In marriage, a woman's sexuality is not her own but is to be guarded for use by others. A violation of women's sexuality is not so much a violation of another adult's choice to participate in sexual relations outside the socially condoned arena, but rather the violation of property properly belonging to another man (father, brother, husband). In most societies, a rape devalues a woman socially, and her own suffering and pain is of secondary concern in the society's eyes.

* Wendy Harcourt completed her PhD on 'Medical discourse relating to the female body' in 1987. She now works in Rome, Italy as editor of *Development*, Journal of the Society for International Development, and as Senior Programme Officer where her current programme interests are in gender, development and environment.

19

If we are to understand better the ideology underlining sexual relations which continue to determine women's identity, social status and quality of life, women of all cultures need to speak more openly of their experiences in early family life, of the pleasures and difficulties of their adult life, of expectations of their sexual choice. We need to recognize that sexuality is a powerful component in all societies, albeit expressed differently, but that across cultures family structures are based on inequitable sexual relations which do not just confine themselves to the private arena.

If we are to seek the social and economic development of society we must also seek such fundamental human rights as women's freedom to express their own sexuality and creativity in work and in the home, in and outside the family, unimpaired by sexual harassment and violence, and empowered to choose their way of life as freely as men. The family could play an important role in changing the conditions in which women work and live.●

MOTHERHOOD AND MOTHERS □

Becoming a mother is an astonishing event and one which very many women regard as the most important in their lives. The relationship between mother and child is uniquely different to all others. Motherhood has been described as every woman's true destiny, her primary goal in life and her sole means of achieving fulfilment as a human being.

The ideal of the perfect mother is strong in every culture; for example, the Madonna and Child image is prominent in Christian iconography. Motherhood is surrounded by mystique, extolled in legends, poetry and theatre. Motherhood is an important path to social status and personal achievement.

Children are widely regarded as a great gift and a blessing: they continue the family line and preserve property and wealth. Sons, in particular, are a sign of future prosperity, whilst all children offer the hope of achievements unattained by their parents. They also help to fulfil women and men's needs for emotional support and companionship. Pressure to have children is also strong. Children are widely regarded as cementing the relationship between their parents and as bringing economic and emotional security for the future.

For women in low-income households in Africa, Latin America, the Caribbean and Asia, children are a source of additional labour power, security in old age and status. Where poverty, disease and lack of services result in high infant and child mortality, where one child in three will not reach her or his fifth birthday, couples have many children to compensate for those who will not survive. Each year, 14 million children die from common illnesses, usually combined with some degree of malnutrition.

Children's labour is one resource over which women have some control. From an early age, children are allocated numerous tasks. Young girls assist in collecting water, fuel and food. Girls and boys help in farming, selling food or other products in the nearby market or in urban areas. Children represent the only form of security to parents in old age in most Southern countries. It is estimated that by the year 2000 only 23 per cent of men and 6 per cent of women who are earning wages are likely to be eligible for pensions. Some writers are now questioning if considerations of security in old age are significant in family planning decisions.

Motherhood brings new or enhanced authority within the home. Mothers are responsible for most day-to-day decision-making about the child's care, health, socialization and education, although cultural norms dictate the scope and boundaries of this authority. In some societies fathers generally play a very minor role in child-rearing decisions, for example in the Caribbean, whilst elsewhere their role is

PHOTO: JENNY MATTHEWS

Women are still largely responsible for the care of children: a young Dao woman with her son in Quang Ninh Province, Vietnam.

much greater; women's authority varies accordingly. Furthermore, children can offer considerable emotional support to women. In all societies children are a source of prestige and bring new standing. Motherhood is socially acceptable; in some European countries, for example, young unemployed teenagers see motherhood as a way to gain some status. Research from India shows that young brides have no influence or even means of communication within the family until they have borne several children:

The child is her saviour, in a way, instrumental in winning her special status, love and acceptance from others.[11]

Fatherhood too, is looked on with approval by parents, employers and the community as a sign of maturity and reliability. To father many children is seen as proof of a man's virility and thus enhances his social position.

HEALTH WARNING One woman dies every minute from causes related to pregnancy

and childbirth, that is, half a million women each year. Over 99 per cent of these maternal deaths, all but 6,000, take place in developing countries. In Asia one-third of one million women die each year, 75 per cent of them in Bangladesh, India and Pakistan; in India, more women die from pregnancy or birth-related causes in one week than in Europe each year. The majority of the remaining deaths are in Africa.[12]

Most of these women are poor and it is an international scandal in the late twentieth century that the act of becoming a mother should continue to jeopardize women's lives. Until recently, maternal mortality received relatively little attention from medical services, national governments or the international community. In many cases where records are inadequate a woman's death is not recorded at all, or if it is, the causes are not given.

In 1987, eight international agencies launched the Safe Motherhood Initiative in an attempt to reduce the number of maternal deaths worldwide by half by the year 2000. The following priorities were identified:

MATERNAL MORTALITY - WORLD HEALTH ORGANIZATION REGIONAL ESTIMATES (Maternal deaths per 100,000 live births)

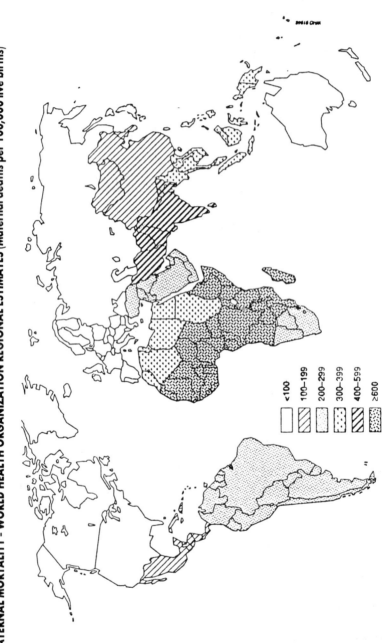

<100
100–199
200–299
300–399
400–599
≥600

The designations employed and the presentation of material on this map do not imply the expression of any opinion whatsoever on the part of the World Health Organization concerning the legal status of any country, territory, city or area or of its authorities, or concerning the delimitation of its frontiers or boundaries.

Source: *Safe Motherhood Newsletter*, Issue 8, March-July 1988.

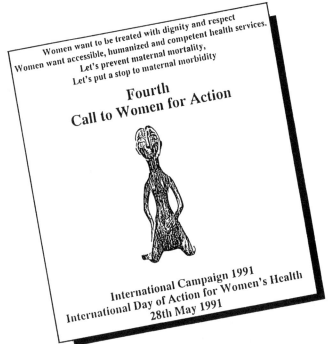

Women want to be treated with dignity and respect
Women want accessible, humanized and competent health services.
Let's prevent maternal mortality,
Let's put a stop to maternal morbidity

**Fourth
Call to Women for Action**

International Campaign 1991
International Day of Action for Women's Health
28th May 1991

- improved socio-economic and political status for girls and women;
- appropriate family planning services for all;
- high quality pre-natal and delivery care for all women;
- skilled obstetric care for high-risk and emergency cases.

Since 1988, women's groups and organizations around the world have set aside 28 May as an international day of action for women's health. This day is marked by protests and demonstrations, publicity events, and lobbying actions to highlight the 'social irresponsibility and negligence' which results in so many women dying each year.

CAUSES OF MATERNAL MORTALITY The chief medical causes of maternal deaths in countries that have very high maternal mortality rates are haemorrhage, often with anaemia as an underlying cause, and sepsis; both of these have become rarities in the North. The World Health Organization (WHO) has estimated that over 95 per cent of rural African women are anaemic. Genital

mutilation can also lead to fatal complications in childbirth, while complications following unsafe abortion are estimated to cause 50 per cent of maternal deaths in Latin America. These medical causes of death disguise the underlying reasons why so many women die: the political, economic, social and cultural structures of the societies where women are living and the discrimination they face at every level. Inadequate diet combined with heavy work and scarce health services damage the health of the woman and the child. The United Nations Children's Fund (UNICEF), the WHO and the United Nations Population Fund (UNFPA) refer to the 'vicious cycle of malnutrition'. If a woman is overworked and malnourished while she is pregnant she is more likely to have a small, weak baby which, particularly if it is a girl infant, may never catch up (see Chapter 5).

Taboos surrounding food are common in many societies and mainly affect women and girl children. These taboos can cover the full range of the most nutritious foods. While the basis for such taboos is usually forgotten, they still carry the full weight of tradition;

they are passed from one generation of women to the next and their transgression is unthinkable for many women. Pregnancy is the subject of many taboos so at their time of greatest need women can be deprived of the foods that are most rich in protein, calories and other nutrients.

As well as being a tragedy in its own right, a woman's death has immediate and long-term implications for the lives and well-being of her children and other family members. Royston and Armstrong point out that the figures for maternal mortality do not tell the full story:

Though exact figures are not known, it is thought that, for every woman who dies, about sixteen women suffer damage to their health which may last the rest of their lives. Some forms of maternal morbidity cause untold misery to individual women and their families.[13]

The safest period for a woman to bear children, anywhere in the world, is between the ages of twenty and thirty-five years. Early, frequent or late pregnancies can be fatal.[14] The level of danger is determined by the health status of the woman and the health services available to her.

TEENAGE PREGNANCY Worldwide, there are about 1 billion teenagers and each year 15 million of them become pregnant. The great majority of young mothers in Asia, Africa and Latin America are married, but there is a significant number of unmarried teenage mothers in other regions, for example, the Caribbean, North America and parts of Europe.

Many factors encourage teenagers to become sexually active, including mass media, changing family patterns and social mores, education and urbanization. Sex education, whether within the family or community or in formal education, is everywhere limited by religious and social taboos; it rarely reflects changing attitudes

and situations. Where contraception is unknown, unavailable or unused, teenage pregnancies are the inevitable outcome with the accompanying serious implications for the teenager's health, physical, emotional and social development. The risks associated with pregnancy and childbirth are much greater in the period before a woman's own body is fully formed: obstructed labour and eclampsia are common complications and can be fatal. Teenagers who want to terminate an unwanted pregnancy opt for abortion, which if illegal is also unsafe.

The social implications of teenage pregnancy can be grave too. Combining full-time education and child-rearing is difficult except where other women in the family can offer full-time assistance. The rate of drop-out from school is high among teenage mothers, whilst stories of their expulsion from full-time education are still common. Teenagers who are already in part- or full-time employment face similar difficulties. Poverty among teenage mothers is high in every country.

Some governments are taking steps to discourage the recent rise in teenage pregnancies. In China, for example, new educational measures have been introduced: in middle schools a course called 'Health Education for Adolescents' on the physiology, psychology and morality of sex has been added to the curriculum. In addition, the government is allowing contraceptives to be sold in drugstores to make them more accessible to adolescents and others.[15]

Measures to improve women's status, for example, equality legislation, access to advanced education and employment opportunities in the modern section of the economy have been shown time and time again to result in later marriage and fewer children. New attitudes to the sex education of girls and boys are also necessary.

HEALTH CARE SERVICES - A PRIORITY
The quality of health care each woman

THE VICIOUS CIRCLE OF MALNUTRITION

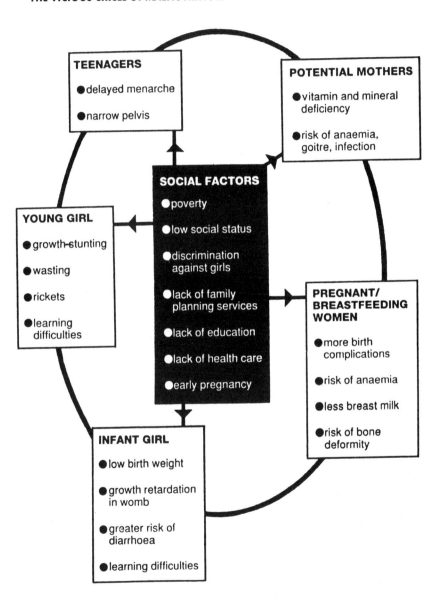

Source: Population Information Program, 1988.

PHOTO: JENNY MATTHEWS

Teenage mothers need special support. At this Jamaican centre for pregnant teenagers, girls can continue their educations during pregnancy.

Teenage pregnancy in Cuba

Cuba is proud of its low birthrate, currently 17 per 1,000 inhabitants – one of the lowest in Latin America and not far behind the industrialized countries (the US rate, for example, is 14 per 1,000). The low rate stems partly from the government's success in improving the status of women. On the other hand, teenage pregnancy and young single motherhood, although not new, are increasingly being identified as social problems.

Ironically, Cuba's teenage pregnancy rate is relatively high for some of the same reasons that the overall fertility rate is low. The revolution has given young women the confidence to claim greater sexual autonomy and choice. It has punctured the traditional obsession with female virginity at marriage. The results: too many teenage pregnancies, a big rise in sexually transmitted diseases such as syphilis and gonorrhoea, and too great reliance on terminating unwanted preg-nancies. Almost a third of all abortions are for women under 20 years old.

Cuba's current priorities are reducing teenage pregnancy and encouraging men to take part in family planning. Its main aim is to increase the use of contraception among young people. Although they know about contraception, only about one fifth of 15–19-year-olds use it. Cuba provides a wide range of contraceptives free or at a nominal charge, publishes sex education materials for different groups and trains medical staff and teachers in communication and advice-giving on sexual issues.

Wider sexual options and fewer restrictions have not radically challenged old patterns of gender relations. Cuban male attitudes echo those found in other parts of the world: the condom is an object of ridicule, diminishing machismo; contraception is not seen as a man's responsibility.

Source: Mandy Macdonald, in *The State of World Population*, New York, UNFPA, 1991

receives is a decisive factor in ensuring healthy pregnancy and childbirth. The basic health needs of the majority, and the particular health needs of women, are rarely given priority in government health spending and thus millions of women have no access to health care services. UNFPA argues that just one antenatal examination could identify three-quarters of women who are at risk and that this could be done even in the poorest countries.

One of the cruel ironies of the late twentieth century is that while millions of women in the South receive no professional health assistance in pregnancy and childbirth, women in the North are campaigning against over-medicalization. While recognizing the specific conditions where technological intervention is beneficial, campaigners in the North argue that the overuse of high-technology scanners and foetal monitors reduces women's power over their own pregnancy and delivery and reinforces the tendency to regard pregnancy as an illness, as a pathological rather than a natural phenomenon.[16]

BREAST-FEEDING AND NUTRITION □

Breast milk is a nutritionally balanced food and therefore the best possible food for babies. It gives protection by immunization, provides anti-bacterial and anti-viral substances, protects mothers against breast and cervical cancer, and reduces exposure to pathogens in the environment. Breast-feeding plays an important part in the bonding of mother and child. By contrast, dried baby milk does not provide disease protection, is not comparable with breast milk in terms of nutrients, is too expensive for many women and can become contaminated because of the problems of access to clean water and difficulties of sterilizing feeding bottles.

Breast-feeding is becoming an endangered practice in both Southern and Northern countries. It would seem that the majority of women in Southern countries breast-feed their infants, but several factors have led to a reduction in breast-feeding. The breaking down of traditional family support structures due largely to rapid urbanization and the separation of home and paid work, misinformation about breast-feeding management, and the aggressive promotion of manufactured baby foods are all instrumental in turning women away from breast-feeding.

Concerned by the effects of the constant downward trend in breast-feeding on infant morbidity and mortality rates, UNICEF and WHO have taken a number of global measures to protect, promote and support the practice. In 1981, 118 states at the

---

The Innocenti Declaration on the Protection, Promotion and Support of Breast-feeding, 1990
- All women should be enabled to practise exclusive breast-feeding and all infants should be fed exclusively on breast milk from birth to 4-6 months of age. Thereafter, children should continue to be breast-fed, whilst receiving appropriate and adequate complementary foods, up to 2 years of age or beyond.
- Efforts should be made to increase women's confidence in their ability to breast-feed. ... [O]bstacles to breast-feeding within the health system, the workplace and the community must be eliminated.
- Measures should be taken to ensure that women are adequately nourished for their optimal health and that of their families. Furthermore, ensuring that all women also have access to family planning information and services allows them to sustain breast-feeding and avoid shortened birth intervals that may compromise their health and that of their children.
- All governments should adopt national breast-feeding policies and set appropriate national targets for the 1990s.
- National authorities are further urged to integrate their breast-feeding policies into their overall health and development policies.

At the Chamanculo Hospital in Maputo, Mozambique, immunization and growth monitoring are used in the revival of community health actions devastated by warfare.

World Health Assembly adopted the WHO Code of Marketing of Breast Milk Substitutes. In 1990 UNICEF and WHO convened a top level policy-makers' meeting in Italy and produced the Innocenti Declaration on the Protection, Promotion and Support of Breast-feeding, which presents breast-feeding as a right of both mother and child and sets ambitious goals and operational targets for 1995.

In September 1990, the World Summit of Children included the goals of the Innocenti Declaration in its 'Goals and Plan of Action'. In 1991, WHO and UNICEF launched their Baby-friendly Hospital Initiative. This recognizes that breast-feeding requires more than a commitment on the part of one woman and her infant:

Breast-feeding is an endangered practice that requires the support of everyone in society to nurture it back it its full, potent strength. It requires a commitment on the part of health care institutions, decision-makers, governments and individuals in the community to ensure a totally baby-friendly environment.

The initiative set out ten steps (see box) which every facility providing maternity services and care for newborn infants should follow in order to promote and assist successful breast-feeding.

Ten steps to successful breast-feeding:

1. Have a written breast-feeding policy that is routinely communicated to all health care staff.
2. Train all health care staff in skills necessary to implement this policy.
3. Inform all pregnant women about the benefits and management of breast-feeding.
4. Help mothers initiate breast-feeding within a half-hour of birth.
5. Show mothers how to breast-feed, and how to maintain lactation even if they should be separated from their infants.
6. Give newborn infants no food or drink other than breast milk, unless medically indicated.
7. Practise rooming-in – allow mothers and infants to remain together twenty-four hours a day.
8. Encourage breast-feeding on demand.
9. Give no artificial teats or pacifiers (also called dummies or soothers) to breast-feeding infants.
10. Foster the establishment of breast-feeding support groups and refer mothers to them on discharge from the hospital or clinic.

Mothers and daughters

All these years
dead and gone
All those words
without meaning . . .
If I knew then
what I think
I know now,
here's what
I hope
I would have said.

Mother,
Why did you pretend
that you were
helpless
when you knew
you could be
strong?
Why did you pretend
that Our Father
was the
Head-of-the-Family
when you knew
that he was not?
And why did you pretend
that He was
omnipotent
when you knew
that your presence
was his strength?
Why did you pretend
that you were
foolish
when you knew
you could be
wise?

Mother,
it's the you
in me
that I resist,
Living your life
inside my own,
Carrying your burdens
and your pain

locked within me,
Trapped in the traps
you set yourself
and us,
your daughters.

Mother,
I can feel
the chainthreads
Pulling me
to you,
you to my
father,
Linking me
with you
and both of us
with both
Our Fathers,
Connecting
each of us
with those
that came
before us.
The chainthreads
of love,
of duty
and devotion . . .
The chainthreads
of anger,
dependence
and oppression . . .

Mother,
it's only now
years later
that I see
your wisdom
your strength
and your power.
Mother,
you were the rock
in our family.

Charmaine Pereira
African Woman,
Winter 1989

A woman must be in a position to make an informed decision about breast-feeding, mindful of her own health and circumstances and the health and well-being of her infant.

The value of breast-feeding should be taught in schools and the appropriate training should be provided for health care workers and maternity staff so that breast-feeding can be successfully initiated and continued. Support groups and counsellors can greatly assist and encourage women. Support structures within the family and the community, the workplace and in society at large would enable women to choose breast-feeding without jeopardizing other priorities, such as earning an income. Along with support, breast-feeding also needs protection in the form of legislation to control the marketing of manufactured baby milks. In Brazil, for example, the national breast-feeding promotion programme showed the greatest gain in breast-feeding rates immediately after a baby milk marketing law came into effect.

REPRODUCTIVE RIGHTS □ The right to control one's fertility is now widely recognized as a basic human right. The importance of family planning to women's general well-being and health is widely accepted. For women with good social, health and financial support, the timing, number and spacing of pregnancies can be unproblematic. For low-income women with limited access to health care, the timing, number and spacing of children create problems for the woman herself, for the baby and for her other children too.

There is overwhelming evidence that women want only the number of children they can care for adequately and educate satisfactorily. Some cite the high incidence of unsafe abortions as an additional indication of women's desire to limit their family size. The desired number of children varies with the mother's social and educational status,

the father's wishes, the stage of economic development, family income and infant mortality rates. In very many cases, women have more children than they desire, for many reasons including failure of traditional birth control methods, pressure from husbands, desire for a son. Millions of women have no access to safe, appropriate, reliable, affordable and easy-to-use contraceptive or other fertility regulatory methods.

The most recent statistics indicate that of couples where the woman is in her reproductive years, approximately 45 per cent in the South and 70 per cent in the North are using some form of contraception or traditional regulatory method. The levels vary widely within the South: 14 per cent for Africa; 50 per cent in Asia; and 56 per cent in Latin America. For individual countries in the North, the figure ranges from near zero to 75 per cent.

POPULATION PROGRAMMES Population programmes as carried out in the period from the 1974 Bucharest Conference to the mid-1980s were often the only development programmes directed towards women, but only as mothers or potential mothers. These programmes have been severely criticized: some adopted coercive methods, whilst the policy-makers and practitioners appeared indifferent to the harmful effects of certain contraceptive methods on the 'accepting' women. Abuses in the implementation of the programmes have been well documented.[17]

An important problem with all programmes that aim to reduce fertility is that, because they are encouraged by the Northern donors and promoted by national governments, many of which are not renowned for their evenhandedness, some analysts regard them as motivated by racial and class considerations. The encouragement given to white women in the North to have children, for example the pro-natalist policies in France, has been highlighted by many writers. Mies[18] characterized the logic of the population control establishment as 'eliminate poverty by eliminating the poor'. Akhter[19] talks about a depopulation policy. She argues that Western anxiety over the birth rate in developing countries reflects Western cultural, ideological, and technological imperialism.

Research, and such events as the UN Decade for Women, brought an understanding of women's multiple roles and demonstrated the links between such factors as status, literacy, education, employment, decision-making power and fertility. It became clear that so long as children remained the primary road to social prestige and financial survival, it would be unlikely that small families would be regarded as advantageous or that action would be taken to limit family size.

Recent statements from Dr Nafis Sadik of UNFPA show a deeper approach to the population issue. She speaks of 'widening [women's] choice of strategies and reducing their dependence on children for status and support', of providing not only family planning services but also health and education services, and of removing the barriers that prevent women from exploring their full potential – that is, 'granting them equal access to land, to credit, to rewarding employment – as well as establishing their effective personal and political rights'.[20]

Until very recently men were invisible in family planning target groups, as women were seen as totally responsible for family planning decisions and actions. This approach ignored the power imbalances in gender relations and the necessity of obtaining men's support and participation in family planning. It also missed the opportunity to educate men and promote methods of contraception other than those that involve women only. Kabir suggests that the presence of family planning programmes has actually discouraged male responsibility in planned parenthood by not promoting the old methods of contraception which required

male co-operation such as withdrawal, rhythm or post-partum abstinence, or the male methods such as condoms or vasectomy.[21] There is a much greater emphasis now on involving and educating men.

GLOBAL POPULATION The global population increase in the twentieth century has been unprecedented: in 1900, the global population was 1.7 billion and by 1990 it had risen to 5 billion, mainly as a result of decreasing mortality rates. It has been predicted that, at current rates of growth, the world population will reach 11 billion or more by the year 2020. But a closer look at the population trends, advocated by Kabir,[22] indicates that population has not been growing unchecked. She writes that there has been a sustained transition to lowered fertility rates, leading to bare replacement levels and in some cases declining rates of population growth in many Northern countries, while in the South population growth has also declined in most countries since the mid-1960s, with the exception of sub-Saharan Africa.

In the late 1980s and early 1990s, the environmental crisis coupled with the economic recession focused renewed attention on population numbers. The links between population and environment are the subject of much debate. In the view of Dr Nafis Sadik, speaking at the United Nations Conference on Trade and Development (UNCTAD) VIII in 1990:

If the UN target reduction in fertility - from 3.8 to 3.3 children per woman by the turn of the century - were not achieved, the result would be continuing poverty, increasing damage to the environment, still higher levels of urban growth and increasing pressures towards international migration.

In February 1992, concerned scholars from the Social Science Research Council, the International Social Science Council and

Development Alternatives for Women in a New Era (DAWN) came together in Mexico to consider the evidence for the view that population size is a major cause of environmental degradation. Their joint statement presents a different view. The following is an excerpt:

The current macro debate which portrays population growth as the central variable in environmental degradation is not supported by research findings. Extremes of wealth and poverty, leading to over-consumption by some and the erosion of livelihoods for others, skewed distribution and patterns of human settlement (including urbanization) have a stronger demonstrable relationship to environmental degradation than population size *per se*.[23]

Few deny that population and environment are linked; it is a matter of recognizing the complex relationship between fertility and poverty. Simplistic equations could legitimize coercion. The essential points are that every woman should have the right to make informed reproductive choices and that family planning is not a substitute for alternative development strategies that could provide the basis for greater social and economic well-being.

REPRODUCTIVE HEALTH The appropriateness of any given contraceptive method depends on how it fits within the personal attitudes and motivations of women and men and how easy it is to obtain and use. Dr Senanayake points out that 'the nature, quality and the efficiency of the family planning services are probably of equal importance in determining the acceptability and continued use of a method'.[24] In order to make choices, women and men need detailed information about the range of contraceptive options open to them, their effectiveness and side effects. Such family planning services must be provided in an integrated way as part of health care programmes and within the framework of respect for individual rights.

Reproductive health, that is, the ability to reproduce and the ability not to reproduce, is the aim. Senanayake describes a reproductive health approach as a 'commitment to empower women to manage their overall health and sexuality and increase the participation of women in reproductive health policy and programming decisions'.[25]

Guidelines for the Distribution and Use of Fertility Regulation Methods

The International Women and Pharmaceuticals Project in the Netherlands has formulated guidelines for the distribution and use of fertility regulation methods in consultation with and at the request of women and health groups in Southern countries. The guidelines were discussed with over eighty key policy-makers and health workers worldwide, representing a variety of institutions, views and experiences.

Centred on the needs of the users, the guidelines aim to meet the following criteria:

(a) the need for a free and informed choice of methods;

(b) the provision of balanced, objective information on contraceptive and other fertility regulatory methods;

(c) avoidance of incentives and disincentives which may influence the choice of methods;

(d) a healthcare infrastructure that enables contraceptives and other fertility-regulating methods to be used safely.

Copies of the guidelines are available from WEMOS/Women and Pharmaceuticals, Postbox 4263, 1009 AG Amsterdam, The Netherlands.

A BORTION □ Abortion is probably the single most controversial issue in the whole area of women's rights and family matters. The issue strikes deep at the hearts of women's rights campaigners, religious institutions and the 'guardians' of public morality.

The position of those individuals and organizations who wish to enhance or defend women's reproductive rights is based on the commitment to 'a woman's right to choose'. They argue that this choice – to choose when and if to become a mother, to choose whether or not to continue an unplanned pregnancy – is central to women's quest for equality. This choice is regarded by many as the ultimate test of a society's or government's commitment to women's rights. It is argued that as no contraceptive is absolutely effective, and as those methods that are safest for women's health have the highest failure rates, abortion must remain an inherent part of any comprehensive birth control service for the foreseeable future.[26]

Those who oppose abortion on whatever grounds disagree. Some, who belive that the rights of the foetus take precedence over the rights of the woman, are opposed to abortion whoever has control over the decision. Views differ on the timing of this transfer of rights: the view of the Catholic Church is that the foetus becomes a human being at the moment of conception and that its rights are then paramount; others believe that the transfer of rights takes place at fourteen days. Abortion is thus regarded as killing the unborn child. Others hold the view that abortion could be semi-legalized with the decision fully in the hands of doctors. There is a growing Catholic lobby in the US in favour of making abortion an issue of individual conscience and 'informed choice'.[27]

According to medical opinion, the foetus is incapable of independent extra-uterine life before twenty-eight weeks, although with the intervention of high technology medicine it is sometimes possible to maintain the life of a baby born earlier.

THE ONLY CONTRACEPTIVE For those involved in the debate, abortion is clearly as profoundly unacceptable to those who oppose it as it is fundamentally a matter of women's rights to those who are pro-choice. In reality of course, for the majority of the 40 to 60 million women who each year seek to terminate an unwanted pregnancy, usually at great risk to their own lives, the decision is more likely to be based on necessity and desperation than on any notion of rights. Because of lack of access to reliable and safe contraception or other fertility-regulating methods, abortion remains for many over-burdened and impoverished women the only way of dealing with an unplanned pregnancy. Induced abortion is the oldest and probably still the most widely used method of fertility control. The large proportion of the world's women who lack access to safe procedures performed by professionally qualified personnel under aseptic conditions, and who therefore turn to unsafe abortion, put their health at risk.[28]

LEGAL STATUS In Latin America, where abortion is illegal in most countries or permitted only in very specific circumstances, for example, if the foetus is damaged or in cases of rape, 45 per 1,000 women of reproductive age have abortions; that is, 3.4 million abortions are performed each year. The situation is similar in most sub-Saharan African countries; here again, large numbers of abortions are carried out secretly. In north Africa, as in the Middle East, abortion is strictly limited, except in Tunisia which allows abortion on request within the first three months of pregnancy. The abortion rate is high in most Asian countries regardless of legal status. In Thailand, abortion is an offence except where a doctor deems the woman's health is in danger, or following rape, but there is no definition of 'health'. However, unlawful abortion is widely available: in 1978, the rate was calculated as 37 per 1,000 women of reproductive age.[29] In Singapore, where abortion is legal, the rate was 28.4 per 1,000 women.

Abortion is legal in many European countries, but illegal in Ireland and restricted in Spain. The number of abortions carried out in European countries is small relative to the total number of women of child-bearing age and to the numbers in Southern countries, because of the availability and acceptability of contraception.[30]

Campaigns for the legalization of abortion are growing in many countries but so also are the opposing forces. Health professionals and politicians are beginning to address the issue of abortion in many African countries. In Nigeria, the search is for an abortion policy that will balance the interests of both the pregnant woman and the unborn baby. Okagbue argues that the answer would seem to lie in

. . . a moderate abortion policy which would recognize wider ground than at present, particularly in early pregnancy . . . [such as] number of living children, period of time since the last delivery. contraceptive failure, age, and possibly single status. It is also desirable that legislation should specifically indicate abortion for the preservation of physical and mental health.[31]

In countries where abortion is legal, the anti-abortionists or 'pro-life' campaigners are turning increasingly to legislation, rather than public information campaigns, as a way of restricting abortion and making the availability of safe abortion more and more difficult. In the UK, there have been several attempts to amend the existing legislation. In the US too, the principle of 'a woman's right to choose' and abortion on request is meeting a new wave of opposition. In the Philippines, the pro-life movement is reporting suspected abortionists to the National Bureau of Investigation.[32] Attacks on abortion clinics are becoming commonplace in the US, the Netherlands and in France. The irony in the use of extreme violence to 'protect life' has not gone unnoticed.[33]

INADEQUATE SERVICES In reality the majority of women live beyond the reach of safe abortion provision even in those countries where abortion is permitted on limited grounds. Some governments that have recently legalized abortion have yet to provide adequate services to meet the demand. Many factors hamper women's access: shortage of qualified personnel, especially in rural areas; doctors' or administrators' personal objections to abortion; and women's own inhibitions and lack of information.

Of the 4 to 6 million abortions carried out in 1980 in India, where abortion has been legal on broad social grounds since 1971, only 388,000 were reported as having been carried out in public health facilities. There is still a chronic shortage of trained professionals in the rural areas where 78 per cent of the population live.

Women who are wealthy or have access to financial resources can always obtain an abortion regardless of the law in their country. Even where abortion is illegal or severely restricted, the law is usually open to some abuse, manipulation or interpretation. Some doctors are willing to perform abortions privately and many women travel to another country to obtain an abortion.

LEGAL EQUALS SAFE There is overwhelming evidence that, far from stopping women seeking abortion, restrictive laws or lack of access to professional care affects only the outcome of the procedure. Women are forced to turn to unsafe abortion, and the risk to their own lives is increased by 100 to 500 times compared to women who have access to professional care. Royston and Armstrong point out that legalization has led to a marked decline in the number of abortion-related deaths.[34] Clearly, large numbers of women will continue to turn to abortion, legal or not, until safe, appropriate, affordable and accessible contraception is available and socially acceptable.

ISSUES AROUND HIV/AIDS ☐ It is estimated that worldwide over 8 million women, men and children are now affected by the human immuno-deficiency virus (HIV). HIV and acquired immune deficiency syndrome (AIDS) have presented new and acute dangers to women and to the family. The Society for Women and AIDS in Africa talks about the triple jeopardy facing women: as individuals, as mothers and as carers.

In general, research indicates that women are more likely to be infected by men than men by women. In other words, men appear to be significantly more likely to pass on HIV during unprotected vaginal intercourse than do women.[35] The poor health and social status of most women in lower income groups makes them particularly susceptible to HIV infection. Women's low intake of nutritional foods undermines their immune system and makes them vulnerable to all infections. Furthermore, hierarchical relations between men and women can prevent women from exercising any choice on whether to have intercourse with high-risk partners. The only choice may be between submitting to sex on demand or facing desertion and homelessness. Extreme poverty can drive women into prostitution and therefore increase their risk of contracting HIV. It is estimated that AIDS will kill 1.5 to 3 million women of reproductive age in central and east Africa alone. These women's deaths in turn endanger the lives of their children. Infected women also face the knowledge that they could pass the virus on to their unborn child. There is a 50 per cent chance that a woman who is HIV-positive will infect her child during either pregnancy or childbirth.

Furthermore, HIV infection and AIDS-related deaths impose increased burdens on women: as partners, mothers, sisters, grand-mothers who must care for those with full-blown AIDS; and women have to assume added financial burdens if the men in the family are ill or die. AIDS can destroy families.

People with AIDS and their carers can find their lives disrupted by a devastating combination of economic and emotional pressures. A survey in Zaire showed that, compared with hospital patients without HIV, HIV-infected patients were almost twice as likely to have lost their job, to be divorced or to have moved because of their illness.[36]

Many writers have pointed out that the HIV syndrome is not merely a medical issue, but raises fundamental issues of equity between women and men and between different regions of the world. Decisions about sexual behaviour cannot be separated from the wider social and cultural influences that inform all human behaviour:

Behaviour in its social, economic and political contest is the real challenge of the AIDS pandemic.[37]

It is to be hoped that the new emphasis on safer sex will bring with it a more positive attitude to sexual relations and open up the possibility that sex education may finally receive the priority it deserves. It is a tragedy that millions have to die before we learn good sexual practice.

CONCLUSION ☐ The age at which a woman marries has clear implications for her opportunities for full-time education and for her health and personal development. Legislation to raise the age of marriage is important, but more fundamental are steps to guarantee girls' access to education, which in turn can bring more equality within marriage and open up greater options for women alongside marriage and motherhood. Legislation can play a key role in other areas, for example, in relation to inheritance rights for daughters and widows.

The capacity to give birth is both woman's greatest power and the cause of her subordination. Most societies laud motherhood but deny mothers; the child, especially if it is a boy, is frequently more important than the woman who bore it. It is time that mothers, too, received the support, protection, rights and choices commensurate with the importance of bearing children.

The situation of some women has improved in quite specific ways. Changing social attitudes and greater access to education at all levels, to employment in the formal sector, and to healthcare services and safe contraceptive methods are enabling many women to gain greater control over their lives. There is still much to be achieved. Regrettably, for the majority of women, this change is slow and constantly hampered by poverty and by discriminatory social structures and practices. The allocation of national and international resources to provide appropriate education and health care for women is a crucial first step.

1. In N. Cross and B. Barber (eds.), *At the Desert's Edge: oral histories from the Sahel*, London, Panos/SOS Sahel, 1991, pp. 100-101.

2. C. Moser, 'Gender planning in the Third World: meeting practical and strategic gender needs', *World Development*, Vol. 17, No. 11, 1989.

3. I. Dankelman and J. Davidson, *Women and Environment in the Third World*, London, Earthscan Publications, 1988.

4. C. Oppong and K. Abu, *A Handbook for Data Collection and Analysis on Seven Roles and Statuses of Women*, Geneva, ILO, 1985.

5. M. Mukhopadhyay, *Silver Shackles: women and development in India*, Oxford, Oxfam, 1984, p. 11.

6. E. Royston and S. Armstrong (eds.), *Preventing Maternal Deaths*, Geneva, WHO, 1989.

7. T. Lauras-Lecoh, 'Family trends and demographic transition in Africa', *International Social Science Journal*, No. 126, November 1990, pp. 475-92.

8. Ibid.

9. Ibid.

10. A. Thiam, *Black Sisters Speak Out: feminism and oppression in black Africa*, London, Pluto, 1986, pp. 88-9.

11. S. Bhogle, 'Indian mother', paper presented to the UNESCO International Symposium of Experts on the Changing Roles of Men and Women in Private and Public Life, Athens, Greece, 3-6 December 1985.

12. E. Royston and A. D. Lopez, 'On the assessment of maternal mortality', *World Health Statistics*, Vol. 40, No. 3, 1987, p. 214.

13. Royston and Armstrong, p. 137.

14. Ibid., p. 187.

15. International Planned Parenthood Federation, *People*, Vol. 16. No. 1, 1989.

16. A. Phillips and J. Rakusen, *The New Our Bodies, Ourselves: health book by and for women*, London, Penguin, 1989.

17. For example, B. Hartman, *Reproductive Rights and Wrongs: the global politics of population control and contraceptive choice*, New York, Harper and Row, 1987.

18. M. Mies. *Patriarchy and Accumulation on a World Scale*, London, Zed Books, 1986.

19. Akhter, cited in Spallone, *Beyond Conception: the new politics of reproduction*, London, Macmillan, 1989.

20. Investing in Women: the focus of the '90s. New York, UNFPA, 1990, p. 1.

21. N. Kabir, 'Women and population issues', paper prepared for the Third Meeting of Commonwealth Ministers Responsible for Women's Affairs, Ottawa, 9-12 October 1990, p. 12.

22. Ibid., p. 5.

23. Statement from a workshop organized by the Social Science Research Council, International Social Science Council and DAWN, 1992.

24. P. Senanayake, 'Selection of a contraceptive: what guides a woman?', paper presented to a meeting on Steroid Contraceptives and Women's Response, Harvard School of Public Health, Boston, 21-24 October 1990.

25. P. Senanayake, 'Women's reproductive health – challenge for the 1990s', paper presented to the Society for Advancement of Contraception, Singapore, November 1990.

26. Phillips and Rakusen, p. 314.

27. J. Hurst, *The History of Abortion in the Catholic Church: the untold story*, Washington, Catholics for a Free Choice, 1989.

28. Royston and Armstrong, p. 107.

29. K. Rayanakorn, 'Women and law in Thailand', in *Women's Legal Position in Thailand*, Chiangmai University, Women's Studies Programme, Faculty of Social Sciences, 1991, pp. 20-37.

30. Royston and Armstrong.

31. I. Okagbue, *Studies in Family Planning*, Vol. 21, No. 4, quoted in *WGNRR Newsletter* No. 34, January-March 1991.

32. *Health Alert*, July 1991.

33. G. Ashworth, personal communication, 1991.

34. Royston and Armstrong.

35. Panos Institute, *Triple Jeopardy: women and AIDS*, London, Panos Institute, 1990, p. 13.

36. Ibid., p. 63.

37. Ibid., p. 91.

THE CARING CAREER

Women Work

I've got the children to tend
The clothes to mend
The floor to mop
The food to shop
Then the chicken to fry
The baby to dry
I got company to feed
The garden to weed
I've got shirts to press
The tots to dress
The cane to be cut
I gotta clean up this hut
Then see about the sick
And the cotton to pick

Shine on me, sunshine
Rain on me, rain
Fall softly, dewdrops
And cool my brow again

Maya Angelou[1]

The idealization of the institution of motherhood as all-powerful, strong and caring brings with it the implication that mothers alone have full responsibility for child-bearing and all the related household caring and domestic work.

THIS ALL- AND EVER-COPING IDEAL, reinforced by kinship, state structures, religious institutions and employers, underlines the social and economic policies of most governments who act in only a limited way to protect or support women in their mothering role. No government fully recognizes the needs of mothers or provides satisfactory support structures. Some are making considerable efforts, but in many countries the health- and child-care and other social services have been the first casualties of the economic crisis and recession (see Chapter 6).

Motherhood as defined above is both an honour and a heavy responsibility. It is widely assumed that within families women provide most, if not all, of the practical and emotional support and nursing, as well as general care required by young children and by family members who are ill, disabled or elderly. This is an obligation dictated by custom and convention; it is not always a matter of choice, and consequently it frequently goes unacknowledged. Policymakers, men in the family and most women regard it as one of women's roles. For the most part and within the limitations of economic circumstances, women fulfil these roles well and find them rewarding and satisfying, but often not without high costs to themselves.

On the altar of maternity women have sacrificed many aspects of their lives, accepting their exclusion from various social spheres and taking a series of responsibilities with their husbands and children which should actually be shared with them and other social institutions.[2]

Kin-keeping

There is rather extensive literature showing that women are the kin-keepers, and that their preparation for this role starts early in life. Kin-keeping tasks include maintaining communication, facilitating contact and the exchange of goods and services, and monitoring family relationships. These functions are often performed for the husband's kin as well as for the woman's own family line.[3]

CARING FOR CHILDREN ☐ Caring for babies and young children is one of the most important functions in all societies and cultures. Although it is a pleasurable and rewarding role, it can also be demanding and time-consuming. Child care involves a range of tasks to meet the child's basic needs: feeding, bathing and clothing. It also includes monitoring the child's health, dispensing remedies, worrying when the child is ill and visiting health care professionals. Additionally, child care includes being the child's entertainer and playmate, educator and socializer, source of information, views and values.

In every society, women are the primary carers of children. They are usually responsible for the care and maintenance of all children living with them, including some which may not be their own. It is mostly women who take time off from work and other activities when children or other family members are ill. Men, too, have child care responsibilities, but in practice most men spend very few hours with their children, except in unusual circumstances or following the death of the children's mother. Grandfathers in some societies help to care for young children. Although in Muslim families the custody of children passes to men, usually when boys reach the age of seven and girls nine, women provide the day-to-day care at all ages. Traditionally in some African societies, men have limited responsibilities towards their own children but are required to meet the needs of parents, sisters and brothers and other older family relatives.[4]

Women adopt a variety of methods of caring for their children, usually relying on family solidarity. Those who work in agriculture or the informal sector usually take their infants with them to the fields, the market or the street, while young children are left at home in the care of an older child, young relative or grandmother. Workers in full-time formal sector employment usually have little choice but to leave both infants and young children in the care of older children, relatives or neighbours; otherwise, they must adjust their work schedules, opt for part-time or night work or, in the last resort, give up work temporarily. Women in middle-income social groups frequently employ other women to care for their children and home.

In Northern countries similarly, some women receive child care assistance from other family members; for smaller and more dispersed families such help is often not available. Many women pay others to act as childminder during their own working hours. A significant number of women with young children are at home full-time either from choice or because they cannot find employment or affordable child care.

One English family's child care arrangements:

'Well, my husband comes home at three and I go in at three. We're both off on Mondays; he's off on Tuesdays; I go in Tuesday afternoon; I'm off today. So my mother comes up Wednesdays and Fridays and sits with her – it's only an hour and 20 minutes, you see, from when I leave to when he gets home, so she sits with her for that time. And Saturdays and Sundays, then mum sometimes comes up on Saturdays, but a friend has her on Sundays . . . so it's not too bad.'

(*Guardian*, 4 December 1991)

In some societies, older women take over the child care roles of their daughters and sometimes also the household work. Older women, too, are frequently the traditional birth attendants and the recognized experts on child-rearing.

The practice of fostering children is common in many African and Caribbean countries and elsewhere, and is one way in which child care is shared between women. A relatively wealthy family may rear children

Having tea together offers a chance to talk: Marrakesh, Morocco.

from less advantaged kin; a family with fewer children may taken in others. Children from a rural area may move to a different part of the family in a town in order to complete their education, or alternatively may stay in the rural area with a grandmother or aunt when their parents migrate for employment. Children may be sent to live with and assist an elderly relative. In Lomé one in four children aged 10 to 14 lives in a household other than that of her or his mother.

SOCIALIZATION The family is the primary site where young children learn to become social beings capable of operating effectively in the wider society. Within the family, because of the time women spend with children and their responsibility for preserving and passing on cultural norms, they are the main socializing agents. Grandparents, in particular grandmothers, have an important role too. Through day-to-day contact with the child, information is passed on concerning the behaviour, attitudes and motivations of adults, permissible play, degrees of mobility and freedom, which are all part of the socialization process. Within the family children usually learn the system of values and cultural norms that apply to

each sex in their particular society and how to relate to others outside the family. Gendered identity is also developed within the family, accompanied by the 'appropriate' levels of emotional security and autonomy. The socialization of girls is radically different from that of boys.

Formal education and the mass media have an increasing role in the socialization process and an influence that is not wholly benign. Many writers are critical of the stereotyped female and male images promulgated daily in the mass media, and in particular the cult of 'macho' violence.

CHILD CARE SERVICES The rapid increase in the number of women employed in the formal sector in the North has created a dichotomy in women's lives between child care and paid work, and a high demand for child care facilities. Generally, demand for affordable, high-quality child care far outstrips supply and the capacity or willingness of governments and employers to provide. Some countries, for example Finland and Sweden, have developed comprehensive national systems for child care but elsewhere there is a grave shortage of good facilities.

In the South, too, the increase in formal sector employment for women, for example

---

Training older women in new ways of child care

A number of Golden Age Clubs in Jamaica have combined with the National Council on Ageing and the University of the West Indies to run workshops in new ways of child care for low-income older women aged 60 to 95 years.

The goals of the workshops were to: provide an opportunity for club members to contribute to the care of under-privileged children; to educate club members; and to produce a manual to

train older adults in child care. Activities included making toys from common household scraps of fabric or other materials, learning about childhood development, and discussing home remedies for illnesses typically afflicting children. There were also classes in story-telling. At the end of each two-week training session, the elders received a certificate.

The course highlighted the hidden potential of older women and also lessened the isolation some older women experienced. One graduation class began a study and outreach group of their own.[5]

Convention on the Rights of the Child

On 2 September 1990 the Convention on the Rights of the Child entered into force.

The Preamble to the Convention reaffirms the fact that children, because of their vulnerability, need special care and protection, and it places special emphasis on the primary caring and protective responsibility of the family.

In its fifty-four articles the Convention covers civil, economic, social, cultural and political rights for all persons under eighteen years of age to enable them to develop their full potential.

Article 18 contains the following provisions:

1. States Parties shall use their best efforts to ensure recognition of the principle that both parents have common responsibilities for the up-bringing of the child. . . .
2. For the purpose of guaranteeing and promoting the rights set forth in the present Convention, States Parties shall render appropriate assistance to parents and legal guardians in the performance of their child-rearing responsibilities and shall ensure the development of institutions, facilities and services for the care of children.
3. States Parties shall take the appropriate measures to ensure that children of working parents have the right to benefit from child care services and facilities for which they are eligible.

Speaking on the occasion of the Convention's entry into force, Javier Perez de Cuellar, then United Nations Secretary-General, said: 'The way a society treats its children reflects not only its qualities of compassion and protective caring, but also its sense of justice, its commitment to the future and its urge to enhance the human condition for coming generations. This is as indisputably true of the community of nations as it is of nations individually.'

in the public services and in export-processing zones, combined with urbanization and separation from kin, have created a growing demand for child care facilities and support services. In the Philippines, there is a formal child care system for three- to six-year-olds but it is inadequate to meet demand. The Secretary of the Department of Social Welfare and Development admitted in an article in *Malaya* on 8 May 1990 that 'we need 45,000 day-care places and we only have 11,000'.[6] Five large women workers' and community organizations in Korea published a statement on 8 March 1991 demanding that the government and companies take responsibility for providing cheap child care facilities for 10 million workers' families.[7] In Brazil, there is a huge shortage of public day care: in 1985, 76 per cent of children under six years in the metropolitan areas were not in pre-school facilities.[8]

Even in those countries with good child care systems, there are gaps in the service provided. After-school care is virtually nonexistent; insufficient places exist for children with special needs, for example those who have some disability.

CHANGING ATTITUDES A recent study indicated that 80 per cent of fathers in the pre-1989 West Germany thought that women with young children should stay at home while the father worked. As Jankanish reminds us, there is a long process of education ahead to instil an understanding that child care is also the responsibility of men.[9] Once this obligation is understood, then men, in their roles as trade unionists, employers, politicians, may take steps to

Grandparents are an important part of a child's life: Kuprokoyy, Turkey.

ensure child care receives the priority it deserves. There are two other important aspects in the division of child care. First, the organization of working hours prevents women and men combining professional and family responsibilities with ease. Second, employment and wage discrimination ensures that women earn less than men, and therefore when it becomes impossible to combine caring for children and paid work it is women who, logically, have to choose.

For the immediate future, child care will remain one of women's responsibilities. All efforts, therefore, should be directed to provision of a choice of support and facilities to meet their needs.

CARING FOR OLDER PEOPLE ☐ Very many older women and men are active members of their societies, running community organizations, in full- or part-time employment, providing invaluable care and support to younger and older family members. Others, through illness or disability, cannot care for their own day-to-day needs. As life expectancy lengthens in most countries, so also does the period of time when older people may need care and support. The family support system remains the primary and, in most Southern countries, the only support to older people. The majority of the elderly are women, as are the carers.

An alternative vision of day care

'*Day care centres have an unprecedented opportunity to mould the future generation in an atmosphere of independence, autonomy and creativity.*'

Day care centres should enhance the four levels of relationships of the child:

(a) *sense of self*: each child is unique and should develop a sense of self for him/her to be capable of fighting oppression and inequality as a grown-up,

(b) *mutuality of relationships*: which (especially between male and female) should be based on equality and mutual respect;

(c) *family solidarity*: equality should cut across gender and age; the welfare of one family member should not be at the expense of others;

(d) *ecological balance* (relationship with nature and the environment): the habit of stewardship should be fostered at an early age.

Day care programmes should have *flexibility* – a centre should be built where it is most convenient to users, it should be available at times parents need, and it should cater for mixed ages. Importantly, day care programmes should address not only immediate needs but also strategic gender interests.

'*We should aim for changes in gender relations, for example, setting up the day care centre near the workplace of the father instead of the mother.*'

Day care programmes must have sustainability and continuity. State support is needed to meet the demand but the state must understand the reasons behind day care centres: what is needed is not just the commitment of society but also its conversion – not only with regard to budgeting but also in terms of structural change, for example in areas such as equal pay for women and men.

Source: Jurgette Honculada, a commissioner of the National Commission on Women, the Philippines.[10]

AFTER-SCHOOL CLUB

In the UK, the East London Black Women's Organization (ELBWO) was formed in 1979 in the East End of London because of black women's growing concern about problems faced by their children in the education system. ELBWO provides local services while at the same time it campaigns nationally for improved child care.

Since 1979, ELBWO has run a Saturday school to provide supplementary education to black children in subjects such as English and maths, and also in the culture and history of Africa and the Caribbean. The organization has organized holiday play schemes since 1986 and an after-school club since 1989.

ELBWO's After-school Club caters for children aged five to twelve years. Play workers pick up the children from school and take them to the ELBWO Centre where they remain until their parents come for them at around 6 p.m. The children take part in stimulating activities, such as arts, crafts, mini-research projects, cookery and swimming, and are taken on trips to the library or places of interest.

Source: Angela Mpofu, ELBWO

Taking care of elderly relatives is a duty constantly underscored in education in many cultures and one which is not to be transgressed. It may take the form of sheltering elderly relatives, assigning a young person to the elderly person's home, or remitting money. Except in circumstances beyond their control, migrants continue to fulfil their filial duties.

A GROWING CONCERN Low or no social security protection makes it impossible for many older people to remain financially independent once they are unable to earn an income. Care for older family members is becoming an important issue in many countries. Migration has split up families, and low incomes make it difficult to care adequately for older members. Luiz Ramos, speaking at the 1989 Conference on Ageing, reported that in many Latin American countries the elderly living in multi-generational households are the first to demand formal support from the state because the quality of care which family members can provide is not sufficient to meet their needs.[12] Greater longevity has created new caring needs. With age or illness older people may need more support, including companionship, household work, nursing, accommodation or money; thus heavy demands are made on women's time and energy, and often finances.

The general trend towards women having fewer children is having a profound impact on families' abilities to care for their elderly members: fewer children means greater proportional shares of family support obligations per adult. The one-child policy in China, although an unusual case, encapsulates this problem. There are over 90 million people over sixty years of age in China who traditionally would have been supported by children and grandchildren. As China's social welfare programmes are far from comprehensive, grandparents must compete with grandchildren for a share of income earned by the working parent.[13] Eighty-seven per cent of widows in rural areas are dependent on their children. Remarriage is generally not regarded as socially acceptable for older women.[14]

Rising divorce rates and later marriage age mean that many women have simultaneous caring responsibilities for parents and adolescents. Increasingly also, many more carers are older people themselves, caring for a spouse or parent. It is now possible that a women of seventy may be caring for her mother aged ninety. The new situation has highlighted the care previously provided by women, as a matter of course, to older family members. Older family members in turn offer assistance: even if the

PHOTO: UNICEF/HORST CERNI

Chinese one-child family proud of their son.

elderly and their families do not live together, older persons typically live in close proximity to at least one child with whom they exchange many services and other forms of support.[15]

It is estimated that 25 per cent of women aged forty-five to fifty-four in the UK are caring for chronically ill relatives. Before 1989, in the former West Germany, 75 per cent of carers in two-person elderly households where one needed care were women. In Japan, nine times more elderly people with severe disabilities are cared for at home than are cared for in institutions.

CHANGING ATTITUDES Japanese culture places a strong emphasis on mutual help among blood relatives and as a result the proportion of older women and men living with their children (60 per cent of those aged sixty-five and over in 1989) is very high compared with European countries. This proportion was higher but has declined steadily since the 1960s due partly to migration but also to rising numbers of unmarried older people and childless people.

There is also a desire on the part of both young and old to live separately. Most important, the traditional care-givers, married mid-life women, are increasingly in paid employment. Younger women with higher education and those in 'love matches' are less likely to hold traditional attitudes towards family care.[16]

PLEASURES AND PAINS Most women and men are happy and willing to care for elderly parents and relatives and see this work as reciprocating the care they themselves received in childhood. But caring can also be burdensome, tiring and depressing. Carers can suffer enormous stress and isolation and jeopardize their own employment and future economic security for the well-being of elderly relatives. An article in the US magazine *Newsweek*, on 16 July 1990, entitled 'The Daughter Track' reported that in recent years about 14 per cent of women caring for elderly relatives in the US have switched from full- to part-time work and 12 per cent have left the workforce.

Caring for dependent elderly family

In Korea, selected women and men each year are awarded a Filial Piety Award. In one study of 817 women and men, 67 per cent of whom were women and almost two-thirds from low-income families, each person demonstrated long years of pious service, physical, social and financial loss and deprivation of personal well-being. Most cared for seriously impaired elders, 65 per cent of whom were widows. Sons provided emotional and financial support; daughters provided the day-to-day instrumental care, such as bedside nursing. Their motive was respect for parents and a strong sense of responsibility. The rewards were primarily psychological - family harmony - but also some social recognition and praise from neighbours.[11]

members can create tensions between the carer and her or his spouse and children, who may feel neglected and may not be as tolerant as the carer towards the older relative. Tensions within the wider family may also emerge if the carer feels that others are not taking their share of the workload and responsibility.

Because caring is regarded as women's natural role, women tend to get less support from outside agencies than men. Research from the UK has indicated that men carers are more likely to receive higher levels of home help services than women carers, and at an earlier stage in the caring. Also, a severely impaired older woman cared for by her son is more likely to be admitted to residential care than one cared for by her daughter.[17]

CARING FOR THE CARERS Recently more attention has been paid to the needs of carers. The Kitakysushu City Declaration which came from the United Nations Conference on Ageing in 1989 addressed the issue of the impact of caring on the lives of the carers:

...policies should be developed to ensure that family care for the aged: (a) does not hamper gains in women's status or the range of opportunities open to them; and (b) shall be voluntary on the part of both informal providers and recipients, but does not absolve society of its responsibility for high-quality care.

With the current shortage of young workers in some Northern countries, many more companies may be forced to adopt such policies in order to retain women workers. Sixty per cent of the growth in the US workforce in the 1990s will be made up of women aged thirty-five to fifty-four - the group with the most child care and elder-care responsibilities.[18] Yet the perception of women as care-givers is deeply entrenched in US society as in all others. To date, only about 3 per cent of US companies have policies that assist carers. For example, the Stride Rite Corporation opened the US's first on-site inter-generational day care centre catering both for the children and the elderly relatives of employees. Other companies have started support programmes and educational sessions for workers with caring responsibilities.

Carers must be enabled to fulfil their family responsibilities without jeopardizing their own health, well-being and financial security. Care-givers need flexibility in the workplace and time off to care for sick relatives. They need referral and information services, supportive community services, such as home help, day care and respite care - for example, one day off per week and a few weeks off each year when someone else takes over the role of carer, and financial allowances. Most important, male family members must be willing to assume an equal share of day-to-day caring for elderly relatives, a willingness that requires both a change in attitude and the fundamental reorganization of employment in the formal sector.

A new methodology

The Family Programme of INDEX, an NGO started in 1985 in the Philippines, aims to combine family development with women's rights. It believes that the 'family need not become a casualty of the movement towards social progress'.

INDEX's vision is the empowerment of communities based on the transformation of their constituent families. It seeks to develop an organizing methodology that connects the process of community empowerment with the process of family transformation. This involves participatory and collectivized action on the felt needs of the community and a structural analysis of community realities. Added to this is a deliberate programme of consciousness-raising on the relationship between the structures and processes in the home and the structures and processes in the community at large.

INDEX wants to motivate women to become community leaders. Programmes to build women's confidence in responding to both home and community responsibilities are run alongside other activities in health care, training and education which are initiated by the core group of women as needs are identified and appropriate capabilities developed. Sessions are later held involving husband–wife and parent–child dialogues to bring about a more just sharing of responsibilities within the family.[19]

DOMESTIC WORK □ Side by side with the hours they expend to ensure that children, the aged and the ill are well cared for, most women carry out a vast range of unpaid domestic labour. Over and above the fact that many women simply have too much to do, there are two main and closely related problems associated with domestic work: first, the fact that it is done mostly by women, and not men or boys and, second, that it is low-status work.

There is enormous variety in the division of labour between women and men from one society to the next, but broadly speaking the responsibility for domestic work – cooking, washing and so on – rests primarily with women regardless of the income they earn. It may be said that men have a personal investment in holding firmly to the conviction that domestic work is women's domain, but many women also are committed to this view. Most men are trained from infancy to depend on women for the satisfaction of their basic needs for food and comfort. Some women, for their part, vigorously defend their roles, as the house-

hold is the realm in which they exercise considerable authority and expertise. Others accept the situation with a mixture of fatalism and resentment. Many women and men tend directly or indirectly to discourage young boys from taking on domestic tasks.

Divisions of labour exist also among men themselves and among women. Mackintosh, writing about Senegal, gives an example of the social divisions of labour between women. She writes that domestic work is done only by women who are wives or daughters. For example, in polygamous households, the first wife takes over the work of her husband's mother, freeing the older woman for rest or extra income-earning. When the man marries a second woman, the wives usually rotate domestic work (but not child care). As a general rule, other adult women in the household, such as relatives of the household head, do no domestic work.[20]

Most men do some domestic labour. In Cambodia, collecting fuelwood is the responsibility of women but is often shared with children and men. Women weave palm

Minata's Song

We worked together to gather stones
We made a dam;
All the men who travelled to Mecca
say they gathered stones to throw
at the evil tombs of disbelievers
Like them, we gathered stones
But we were going to build a dam,
A future for our children, our village
for Burkina Faso and all of Africa.

Composed by Minata, leader of the Somiaga women's group, Burkina Faso. Reprinted from *Ecoforum*, August–October 1986.

leaves to repair the house and men fix them. Children and men assist in foraging for food each day.[21] In those Muslim countries where women's mobility outside the home is limited, men are responsible for shopping. Men can also be responsible for growing or buying certain products, for example millet, the subsistence crop in rural Senegal.

LABOUR-SAVING DEVICES It is widely assumed by development planners that simple technology at its best and most appropriate, such as improved stoves and bakeries, hand pumps, grinding mills or oil processing presses, should lessen the workload of women in rural areas and enable them to devote more time to growing more food and earning more cash income. However, the reality is more complicated. Carr and Sandhu ask if the use of domestic work-related technology will allow women to generate enough income to pay back the loans needed to acquire the technology in the first place.[22] To date very few case studies have suggested a positive answer to this question.

Whilst labour-saving devices liberate women from certain aspects of domestic work, they do not challenge the sexual division of responsibility and labour or directly improve women's status within the family.

LEGISLATING FOR CHANGE Some governments have attempted to change relations between women and men within the household. Article 28 of the Cuban Family Code, which went into effect in March 1975, stated that both partners 'must participate, to the extent of their capacity or possibilities, in the running of the home, and cooperate so that it will develop in the best possible way'. This declaration, and others like it, do not assume immediate change but they do publicize domestic work, elevate its importance, and give it legitimacy as a political issue.

LOW-STATUS WORK OR LOW-STATUS WORKERS? The second problem associated with domestic work, and one that is a direct result of modernization and monetarization, is that it is undervalued by most women and men and is unvalued by economists. It is widely regarded as unskilled, menial and tedious and its performance is taken for granted by male household members and the wider society. Women's own low status is the deciding factor in determining the low standing of domestic work.

This transferred low standing of domestic work was, and is continually, reinforced. The United Nations System of National Accounts (SNA), the system of economic measurement used in most countries, though

e domestic work continues even in times of distress: Croatia.

with qualifications, attributes no value to women's unpaid work. Thus, whilst child care, cooking or cleaning done by a paid worker is counted, wherever it is carried on, the same work done at home by women or men is not. In some countries, a woman producing food for her family's consumption is regarded as non-productive; when she sells her surplus crops in the local market she immediately becomes economically active.

This classification as non-productive or non-market, and therefore valueless, is critical in an international system which to a great extent recognizes only monetary or market values. Down-valuing domestic work has serious social and economic policy implications. The valuelessness of the work is in turn transferred back to women, as uncounted work means uncounted workers. Waring writes that this makes it impossible to prove to politicians that, for example, child care facilities are needed. She explains:

'Non-producers' (Housewives, mothers) who are 'inactive' and 'unoccupied' cannot, apparently, be in need. They are not even in the economic cycle in the first place. They can certainly have no expectation that they will be visible in the distribution of benefits that flow from production.[23]

In order to end this invisibility, many researchers and campaigners have estimated the value of women's unpaid work, calculated on the basis of the hourly rates of earnings for the same jobs when done outside the home; they have thus drawn attention to the large contribution women's unpaid work makes to each country's gross domestic product.[24] The organizations that have campaigned for many years under the 'Wages for Housework' banner have achieved considerable success in highlighting women's unpaid labour.

There are ideological as well as practical problems in putting a monetary value on work done outside the marketplace and within a totally different ethical framework. The concept of working for ends other than personal financial gain should be reinstated and valued rather than weakened. Measuring women's unpaid work and thereby demonstrating the significant contribution women make to the smooth running of social and economic organizations is an important step in this direction.[25]

Goldschmidt-Clermont is in no doubt that unpaid work must be counted and that having data available that is compatible with national accounting practice is the first step towards revising the SNA. Domestic activities, in her view, are sufficiently significant to justify being handled in their own right, and the problems of evaluation are in no way insurmountable. Furthermore, these activities not only make a significant contribution to the family's total 'income', but in fact are the difference between surviving or not surviving. It is only by formally recognizing the economic value of domestic services, and official measurement of this value, that economic development policies will recognize the need to act simultaneously on the generation of monetary income and on the provision of market substitutes for non-market goods and services.

Some *employment policies*, in particular those intended for women, assume the existence of a labour surplus which is not confirmed by time-use data. Simply to raise monetary income by providing job opportunities that increase the market workload without reducing the non-market workload is damaging from the point of view of welfare.[26]

Considerable strides towards developing systems of measurement for women's unpaid work have been made. Time-use studies are favoured by many researchers as the most comprehensive method; all activities paid and unpaid, including domestic work, caring, community and leisure are recorded.

WOMEN IN MOST REGIONS SPEND AS MUCH OR MORE TIME WORKING THAN MEN WHEN UNPAID HOUSEWORK IS TAKEN INTO ACCOUNT

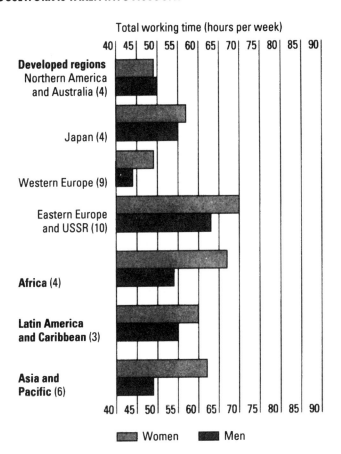

Note: Numbers in parentheses refer to the number of studies in each region.

Source: *The World's Women: Trends and Statistics 1970-1990*, New York, United Nations, 1991. Data are averages from studies in each region, 1976/88, compiled by the Statistical Office of the United Nations Secretariat.

Interesting pilot studies have been carried out in several countries, but there is still a need to find agreed concepts and definitions in order to enable international comparisons to be made.[27]

The policy implications of the valuation of women's unpaid work are immense, for example, in the fields of child care, care for the elderly, family and voluntary health care, social security and pensions and the organization of paid work and personnel policies.

CONCLUSION ☐ The direct result of the sexual division of labour is that most women have too much to do. United Nations statistics have to be restated: in low-income

Family-life Education

In most societies, the majority of family units 'get on with it', carrying out the various functions assigned to the family, including education and socialization. Their level of success is determined by their ability to deliver sane, balanced human beings that are able to cope, become productive members of society, perpetuate the species and carry on cultural traditions.

Given its importance, there is relatively little formalized family-life education. In general, norms, attitudes and behaviour patterns are transferred through non-formal methods and cultural traditions. Social institutions such as the school and church play important roles in this process and reflect a need for more structured interventions to ensure that certain skills are passed on.

Family-life education programmes vary, but in general focus on parenting skills. They try to inculcate sex education, and the importance of love, affection and security for children, and include early childhood stimulation and child care skills. They also cover skills such as family budgeting and career planning and try to teach problem-solving skills. They try to counsel on issues such as child abuse, rape, incest and other forms of violence in the family. Some attempt to address sex role relations in the family to help couples understand social interaction and human relations, and suggest support systems that can be used especially for single mothers. These programmes are deliberate attempts to pass on to the younger members of society cultural traditions relating to the family as well as useful and practical hints that build confidence in doing what should come naturally.

Family-life education programmes also serve as a forum for critically assessing traditions. It is important to analyse the family today and to encourage thinking and behaviour more in line with the needs of contemporary society.

Approaches to family-life education

Sistren, a women's theatre collective in Jamaica, organizes community workshops using drama as a tool for reflection and action. Sistren helps community groups to analyse social problems, particularly those related to women. Their plays on social issues have included *Bellywoman Bangarang*, which deals with teenage pregnancy. Skits, based on real-life experiences, are used to lead workshops. These workshops, plays and their books, which focus on adolescent fertility, family-life education and women's issues, represent a unique approach to family-life education. Special programmes with teenage women provide a supportive environment for analysing traditional sex roles and male–female relationships and encouraging attitude changes that will benefit women. Cultural songs and games are used to create a relaxed and entertaining atmosphere for discussing complex issues.

St Michael's is a private charity in south London, UK, which offers simulated training in parenting skills and helps young mothers to cope with the complexity of adolescent development as well as with being parents. The women and their babies live in separate flats in a large house. They are supervised by trained social workers who teach them basic parenting and child care skills while preparing them to become independent.

During a six- to twelve-month period, assessments are made to determine whether the young mother will be able to cope on her own or the child should be referred for adoption or fostering. Other survival skills taught include household budgeting and time management. The women are also encouraged to complete their education. Visits from the children's fathers are welcomed but they are not allowed to sleep or live there.

The St Michael's programme provides a supportive environment in which vulnerable young women learn coping skills that they were unable to learn through their families.

Source: Leith L. Dunn, a Jamaican sociologist. She is currently researching women's organizing strategies in the context of export-oriented industrialization in the Caribbean.

households, women work on average sixteen hours each day with little or no relaxation time.

Sole responsibility for caring for children, older people, the sick or disabled, combined with domestic work, is a major barrier to women's equality; this is because of the time and energy it demands and the consequent stereotyping of women's capacities. Policy-makers know the facts: there are plentiful references to the 'double burden' and women's low status within the family; they also acknowledge that women have a central role in all social and economic development. Whilst many make the connection they remain uncommitted to the social and economic restructuring necessary to change the status quo. Women have not yet gained full acknowledgement for their enormous contributions; they have not received the support services to enable them to carry out the roles allocated to them; they have not been guaranteed equal pay and treatment in employment and social security. Except in a minority of cases, there is little sign of men offering to assume more family respon-sibilities.

A mammoth programme of re-education of women and men is required to value the day-to-day aspects of human care and maintenance and to ensure this value is reflected in all aspects of social and economic policy and particularly in the organization of paid work.

1. M. Angelou, 'Women Work', in *And Still I Rise*, London, Virago, 1986.

2. C. E. Florez, *The Demographic Transition and Women's Life Course in Colombia*, Tokyo, United Nations University, 1990.

3. G. O. Hagestad, 'The family: women and grandparents as kin-keepers', in A. Pifer and L. Bronte (eds.) *Our Aging Society: paradox and promise*, New York, Norton, 1986.

4. T. Lauras-Lecoh, 'Family trends and demographic transition in Africa', *International Social Science Journal*, No. 126, November 1990, pp. 475–92.

5. J. Sokolovsky, 'New roles for older persons', in I. Hoskins (ed.), *Coping with Social Change: programs that work*, Acapulco, American Association of Retired Persons, 1990.

6. ANAK (Service Program for Alternative Child Care in the Philippines), *Proceedings of the Consultation of Non-government Organizations on Day Care in the Philippines, 27–29 September 1990*.

7. *Asian Women Workers' Newsletter*, June 1991.

8. A. M. Goldani, 'Changing Brazilian families and the consequent need for public policy', in *Changing Family Patterns,*

International Social Science Journal, No. 126, November 1990, pp. 523–37.

9. M. Jankanish, 'Responding to the child care needs of working parents: an overview', in ILO, *Conditions of Work Digest*, Vol. 7, No. 2, 1988.

10. From a talk given at the Consultation of Non-government Organizations on Day Care in the Philippines, 27–28 September 1990. In ANAK.

11. M. J. Gibson, 'West meets East at UN conference on ageing and the family – report on conference', *Ageing International*, June 1991, pp. 33–42.

12. Ibid., p. 36.

13. *UNESCO Sources*, No. 24, March 1991.

14. M. J. Gibson, 'Care-giving in Asia', *Network News*, Vol. 5, No. 2, 1990, pp. 1–6.

15. M. J. Storey Gibson, *Older Women Around the World*, International Federation on Ageing in cooperation with the American Association of Retired Persons, Washington, DC, 1985.

16. Gibson, 1991, p. 34.

17. M. Coopmans, A. Harrop and M. Hermans-Huiskes, *The Social and Economic Situation of Older Women in Europe*, Brussels, Commission of the European Communities, quoted in *Ageing International*, June 1990.

18. US Bureau of the Census, *An Aging World*, 1987.

19. INDEX, 'Family-based community organizing: an exploration', *Family Development*, Vol. 1, No. 2, January 1990. Quezon City, Newsletter of Social Development Index, pp. 2ff.

20. M. M. Mackintosh, 'Domestic labour and the household', in S. Burman (ed.), *Fit Work for Women*, London, Croom Helm, 1979.

21. B. Sonnois, 'Women in Cambodia: overview of the situation and suggestions for development programmes', Redd Barna, Consultant's Report, July 1990.

22. M. Carr and R. Sandhu, 'Women, technology and rural productivity: an analysis of the impact of time and energy saving technologies on women', unpublished paper for the Intermediate Technology Development Group, Rugby, UK, 1987.

23. M. Waring, *If Women Counted: a new feminist economics*, London, Macmillan, 1989.

24. See, for example, S. Lewenhak, *The Revaluation of Women's Work*, London, Croom Helm, 1988.

25. M. Mies, '"Moral economy": a concept and a perspective', draft paper presented to the Conference of Socialist Economists, London, 10–12 July 1992; and M. Mellor, *Breaking the Boundaries: towards a feminist green socialism*, London, Virago, 1992.

26. L. Goldschmidt-Clermont, *Economic Evaluation of Unpaid Household Work: Africa, Asia, Latin America and Oceania*, Geneva, ILO, 1987.

27. Papers submitted to the Work Session on Statistics and Women organized by the United Nations Statistical Office and the Economic Commission for Europe, Geneva, 27–29 April 1992.

ECONOMIC RELATIONS AND REALITIES

The evidence from many countries indicates that women do have a real need for income and that the ideal of men as sole providers for women and children is a myth. The inadequacy of male incomes is a fact of life for the majority of Third World households as is the importance of women's earnings to the survival of many families.[1]

IN LOW-INCOME HOUSEHOLDS, women's earned income and their ability to stretch this and other resources is vital to the survival of many households. Thus, whilst access to and control over the disposal of cash is an issue in all households, it can become the cause of acute power struggles between women and men when income is scarce and the welfare of household members is at stake. When cash is short, the stress of coping falls disproportionately on women, who are likely to deny their own needs in the interests of others.

HOUSEHOLD NEGOTIATIONS □ The family home can be the site of considerable authority for women; they manage the household, guide the children and foster relationships with kin and community. However, this household authority appears to have limited influence when it comes to relations with men. Whilst in many households all income is pooled and women are the recognized money managers, it is now widely recognized that within each household unit, adult women negotiate, overtly or covertly, about a range of decisions including how money is spent. This negotiation, which can involve amicable trade-offs and intense struggles, is primarily with husbands, but depending on the cultural setting it may also be with parents, in-laws, siblings and children. Other 'commodities', too, can be the subject of negotiation, such as children, labour, sexual relations or care of in-laws.

It is no longer credible to use the household as the basic unit for data collection or to assume that adult males are the household heads and that by interviewing them one learns all about the sources and overall levels of household income and the welfare of all household members. Dwyer and Bruce stress that to see the marital relationship as 'a sanctum protected from the conflicts that characterize virtually all other social institutions' is implausible:

... since men's and women's access to and control of resources differ systematically in the wider world - the external world of income relations - why would their personal economies be served by a common ground plan in the internal world of income relations?[2]

Sen[3] argues that individuals within the household contend but in many cases cannot bargain in the precise sense of this word because 'the perception of interest is likely to be neither precise nor unambiguous'.[4] He proposes that intra-household negotiations experience 'cooperative conflict' around a number of elements including fundamental survival and individual interests (or welfare) and variables, such as concepts of what is deserved and what is legitimate related to perceptions of who is 'contributing' how much to the overall family prosperity.

Women and men are rarely equal negotiating agents. Women's low status within the family in general, the inequality between women and men, and women's limited opportunities for earning all place them at a serious disadvantage in household economic relations. Men's and women's economic contributions tend to be differentially valued by others and self, a circumstance that generally works to men's benefit. The strength of a woman's negotiating position is related to the level of support from her own natal family, her education and income but also importantly to her self-perception and self-esteem: 'If a woman undervalues herself, her bargaining position will be weaker, and she will be likely to accept inferior conditions.'[5]

SPENDING PRIORITIES In all societies, most women and men have significantly divergent priorities when it comes to expenditure and disposal of cash. In general women devote a far greater proportion of their income to their children's basic needs and interests, whilst men's contributions vary widely. There is wide diversity in cultural rules on the parental responsibilities of fathers and mothers and therefore on the level of shared interests.

Other factors are also important. While the evidence from some studies indicates that when women earn a cash income men often contribute less to the household, other research shows the opposite. In real terms, because men usually earn more, they frequently contribute more than women. However, the proportion of their income that comes into the household budget is usually less than the proportion contributed by women and relates more to the level of their income than to the actual needs of the household's members. Pahl found that in poorer households in England and Wales men contributed more in absolute terms and women contributed more in relative terms:

Put simply, if a pound entered the household economy through the mother's hands more of it would be spent on food for the family than would be the case if the pound had been brought into the household by the father.[6]

There is also a marked difference in the amount of their earnings that women and men spend on their personal satisfaction or leisure. Apparently gender ideologies commonly accept that men 'have a right to personal spending money, which they are perceived to need or deserve, and that women's income is for collective purposes'.[7]

Defending the family income

The Housewives Committee emerged in 1960 in the mining areas of Bolivia when a group of sixty women organized to obtain freedom for their husbands imprisoned for demanding better working conditions. The committee remained a vocal and powerful force until the mid 1980s. The women demanded improvements in public goods and services, such as quantity, quality and cost of foodstuffs; they defended the miners who had been arrested for political and union activities; they organized hunger strikes, demonstrations and protest marches to put pressure on the government and the mining company.

In its most active decades, the committee never proposed autonomy for itself and remained an auxiliary association of the mineworkers' union. The women emphasized alliance with their men against the government and the mining company and attributed their own disadvantages as women to the capitalist exploitation of their country. The closure of most mines in the 1980s and the relocation of thousands of mining families caused the committee to disperse as a national force. The debt crisis forced the housewives to become paid workers and brought new roles and identities.

Based on: Gloria Ardaya Salinas 'The Barzolas and the Housewives Committee', 1986.[9]

This is very much in keeping with women's altruism within the family.

Studies from many regions, for example, from southern Africa, show that many men now fail to contribute financially to the household.[8] Previously under the customary legal systems, husbands and wives, as well as their extended families (ideally), shared the responsibility for maintaining children and each other. The changed socio-economic situation and in particular migration have loosened the father's ties with his children; it seems that men who do not live with their families are less likely to contribute to the needs of the household.

AN EGYPTIAN CASE A study carried out in a low-income neighbourhood in Cairo in 1983–84 illustrates many of the above points.[10] The neighbourhood had developed in the previous twenty years and was made up mainly of first- or second-generation migrants from the rural areas or from other, more densely populated parts of the city. Nuclear-family households were the norm.

Complaints about financial problems with their husbands were the main subject for discussion when women met. In most households the family income only just covered the basic and immediate needs and therefore women's primary concern was more with budgeting than with access to or control over household cash. Women wanted access to financial information as this was seen to militate against excessive expenditure by husbands; the more information women got, the less strife in the household.

There were some household and family items for which men refused to pay, being more likely to buy a television set or cassette recorder than a gas cooker. Some women joined in local savings schemes with friends and neighbours to buy small items for the house, clothes for their daughters, or to pay for children's school fees or presents for their relatives. Women were more willing than men to pay for their children's education and private lessons.

The most visible difference between families in which women had an independent income and those in which they did not was in how women and children were clothed. In most families the men were much better dressed than their wives, especially those who wore Western dress.

There was a great deal of dissatisfaction and resentment about the amount of money men spent on themselves.

He eats chicken and kebab for lunch and dinner; we do not see meat more than once a week. He spends the rest of his time in cafés and cinemas, while we cannot leave the neighbourhood from year to year. He likes himself too much and his needs and comforts come first. I know it is his money, but we are his responsibility.

All the women interviewed held men financially responsible for the household. Yet all but one woman preferred to have their own income.

In households where women had incomes of their own, their husbands contributed only enough for food and rent. Others contributed irregularly. Some paid rent only and occasionally brought items of food and clothing or a present for their wife. Generally, there were fewer arguments when women had some independent income. Arguments were regarded as pointless because the husband would simply leave the house, spend time with his friends, and return only to go to bed. Meanwhile the woman would be left at home upset, and the children would also suffer.

Even in households where men contributed little or nothing, women still continued in the marriage as they saw no alternative. Hoodfar writes:

They explained that a woman's primary desire was to be independent of her parents and to have a home of her own and children. But most women did not earn enough to pay for a home of their own, and even if

they did . . . the community would not accept her. . . . Furthermore, there is a social stigma attached to an unmarried or divorced woman. Even if a woman surmounted these obstacles, she needs to have children, which is impossible outside marriage.

The husbands of most of the women interviewed worked in the modern sector and had adopted the modern value system. This, combined with urban life, made women more dependent on men while men have become more independent from women. According to Hoodfar:

. . . they do not eat at home; they send much of their clothing to the launderette because they claim their wives would ruin it if they washed it. Since they spend very little time at home or in the neighbourhood, they see little reason to spend much of their income at home. Also since they have little respect for the neighbourhood, women cannot organise community pressure to make their husbands conform and pay more money.

The general condition of the labour market, together with the traditional ideology and sexual segregation, has made it difficult for women, particularly those without capital or saleable skills, to gain access to a cash income.

A STUDY IN JAKARTA A study carried out in Jakarta of lower-middle- and middle-income married women ranging in age from twenty to fifty years who were living with their husbands provides a sharp contrast to the above.[11] Here over half the women interviewed made most of the recurrent money decisions but consulted husbands or other family members on large expenditures such as replacing household furniture. There was a clear division of responsibility among household members based on mutual trust and delegation of authority.

Two external factors were seen to influence strongly women's and men's behaviour and strategies in relation to household finances:

first, women in Indonesia have very high levels of participation in the labour market (around 30 per cent) and, second, divorce rates are high (also around 30 per cent). Papanak and Schwede conclude that where divorce and remarriage are frequent it is reasonable for women to develop strategies for the future.

A woman's active role in earning income and managing household finances benefits her family, but it is also of long-term benefit to her personally. She develops the skills and resources to support herself and family members in the event of divorce or widowhood.

THE QUESTION OF MAINTENANCE □ In the following section, Alice Armstrong from the Women and Law in Southern Africa Research Project outlines some of the issues surrounding the role that the law may play in improving the power of women in the struggle for resources within the family. She qualifies her remarks by stating at the outset that there are problems with the legal definition of the family and the concept of marriage because of the contradictions between official and customary law. Furthermore, she adds that even where a 'family' does exist, male migration means that there is little family life in the form of a common household or pooled finances as assumed by the Western legal systems imported to southern Africa.

MAINTENANCE IN SOUTHERN AFRICA: THE RÔLE OF LAW*
Alice Armstrong

There are good arguments for enforcing maintenance laws more efficiently. The first is that it will benefit children. Men have more than an equal share with women of financial resources including greater access

58

to jobs, education, land and so on. Maintenance laws are a way of ensuring that wealth reaching the hands of men will ultimately benefit children.

Second, maintenance laws play an important role in reinforcing men's responsibilities in the domestic sphere. Inequalities in society at large are mirrored by inequalities in the home. For true equality, it is not enough simply to increase women's participation in the public arena, it is also necessary to increase men's participation in the domestic arena. One way of doing this is to reinforce, in law, the ideal that men and women must be jointly responsible for their children. Maintenance laws enforce the financial aspect of this responsibility.

Third, laws requiring men to maintain their families will actually reduce women's dependence on men and therefore increase their power within the home. With an efficiently enforceable right to maintenance from her husband, a woman's power within the home is no longer dependent on her power to persuade her husband to live up to his obligations but includes a legally enforceable right to ensure that he does.

Fourth, enforcing the obligation for men to pay maintenance will increase 'dignity' and 'self-esteem' for women within the marriage situation and after divorce.[a] Giving wives an enforceable legal right to maintenance would save them the indignity of dependence on the whims of their husbands and 'begging' for money. Finally, an effective system of enforcing maintenance obligations may have an important influence on sexual behaviour, particularly the use of contraceptives and family planning.[b] If men were to know that they would have to maintain their children consistently, rather than 'helping out now and then', perhaps they would approve of contraception, particularly in their extra-marital liaisons.

MAINTENANCE FOR WIVES AND EX-WIVES

A more complicated question is raised by the issue of maintenance for wives and ex-wives, rather than merely for children. Over the past several decades a debate on the duty to maintain ex-wives has been raging among feminist scholars.

In southern Africa, women remain financially dependent on men. Women's opportunities in the cash economy are simply lower than men's, and as land formally belongs to men, they can afford to leave the land and go to town, but since women's rights to land depend on their use of it they must stay and farm.

Second, customary laws, except in matrilineal societies in Mozambique and Zambia, are based on the principle that all property belongs to the husband's extended family. As an outsider in this family, the wife is excluded from the benefits of this property. This is particularly evident from inheritance laws, under which the property of a deceased man passes not to his wife but either to his male children or to his brothers.[c] An efficiently enforceable right to maintenance would strengthen a woman's power in this situation, particularly if this right to maintenance were to subsist after the death of the husband.[d]

Finally, in southern Africa women are offered no alternative to being dependent on men. There are none of the state-sponsored social security systems that some Western feminists argue should take financial responsibility, rather than women relying on husbands. Under our socio-economic situation, women are left with no choice.

CONCLUSION

Although there are good theoretical and practical arguments for improving maintenance laws and their efficiency, studies indicate that legal solutions to problems of maintenance may not be appropriate or

---

* A revised version of this article was published in Women and Law in Southern Africa Research Project, *Struggling over Scarce Resources: Women and Maintenance in Southern Africa*, Harare: University of Zimbabwe Press, 1992 and in *Studies in Family Planning*, 23(4), July/August 1992.

effective. Married women may prefer to trade this legal right to maintenance for peace in the home, and/or the social status and other social and economic entitlements that marriage brings (particularly access to land). This trading may also be related to socialization processes which encourage women to be conciliatory rather than confrontational in dealing with people.[c]

Efficiently enforced maintenance laws can, however, be a useful tool for strengthening the power of women within the family. Efficient enforcement means tightening up statutes which may have loopholes allowing men to escape, and training law officials, lawyers, and women in the provisions of the law, particularly enforcement provisions such as orders to pay part of a man's wages directly to the woman.[f]

These measures, when combined with other strategies such as increasing women's education and employment opportunities and improving their legal status in other areas of the law, will improve women's position in society, and in that way contribute to the development of the countries of southern Africa.

a Fastvold and Hellum, 'Money and work in marriage: women's perspectives on family law', *Studies in Women's Law*, No. 26, 1988, Oslo, Institute of Public and International Law Publications Series No. 6.
b See Mbizvo and Adamchak 'Family planning knowledge, attitudes and practices of men in Zimbabwe', *Studies in Family Planning*, Vol. 22, No. 1, 1991, pp. 31–8; and Mason and Taj, 'Differences between women's and men's reproductive goals in developing countries', in *Population and Development Review*, Vol. 13, No. 4, pp. 611–38.
c Stewart, 'Playing the game: women's inheritance of property in Zimbabwe', in A. Armstrong and W. Ncube (eds.), n.d.
d This is the case in Zimbabwe under the Deceased Persons Family Maintenance Act. See Stewart and Armstrong (eds.).
e See Gilligan, *In a Difference Voice: psychological theory and women's development*, Harvard University Press, Cambridge MA, 1982.
f A. Armstrong, 'Maintenance statutes in six countries of southern Africa', in *Working Papers on Maintenance Law in Southern Africa*, Women and Law in Southern Africa Project, Harare, 1990. ●

EARNING AN INCOME ☐ It was recently estimated that, in India, for example, exclusive of their services as mothers and household managers, women contribute 36 per cent of the gross national product. In addition, Dwyer and Bruce argue, women subsidize economic progress in at least four ways: through their underemployment, their unemployment, their willingness to go in and out of the labour market, and their low wages.[12] Adult women of all ages are a growing proportion of the labour force.

Women's income is vital to the well-being of children: child nutrition has been shown to correlate positively with the size of the mother's income; this is not the case for the father's. Income not earned and/or allocated by the woman is not automatically directed towards children's nourishment. Studies from Guatemala in the early 1980s showed that the children of income-earning mothers had more adequate diets at 18 and 30 months than children of the same age of non-earning mothers.[13] A second study from Guatemala found that although the incomes of two-parent households were higher than those of households maintained by women, the amount spent on food was not different.[14] Childless unmarried women also contributed a large proportion of their income to their parents and siblings.

Poverty resulting from declining rural production, male migration, desertion, divorce or widowhood also impels women to join the waged labour force. The 'feminization of poverty' has been noted by analysts since the early 1980s, that is, a situation where women make up the majority of the poor. But dire poverty is by no means the only reason why women work. Work can be a source of satisfaction, independence and liberation for women. More and more women are seeking economic and social independence and self-realization outside the sphere of the family and household. The Commission for Social Development (CSD) writes that: 'women are motivated to work by aspirations for a more meaningful integration into society. In addition, changing attitudes towards the equality of the sexes have also favoured the trend towards paid employment.'[15]

Most women worldwide have to cope with the double burden of domestic work and paid employment. Sorting fish in Luanda, Angola.

SECTORS OF EMPLOYMENT It is estimated that in 1990, 828 million women were regarded as 'economically active', that is, as earning an income. This figure does not reflect the millions of women farmers, domestics, street-traders or unpaid workers in family enterprises. Women's employment or unemployment is universally under-estimated: women's economic activities and hence 'inactivities' are often outside the official system, or women are classified as dependants of income-earning husbands.

Nearly 80 per cent of women in sub-Saharan Africa and over half of women in Asia, excluding western Asia, are farmers. The service sector is a major and growing site of women's employment, especially in the North and in Latin America. Around 71 per cent of women in formal sector employment in Latin America and the Caribbean work in the public service, the retail trade or as domestics. Overall, the industrial sector has the lowest percentages of women workers: 24 per cent in the North; 16–17 per cent in Asia, the Pacific and Latin America; and 6 per cent in Africa. Southeast Asia is an exception; women there account for over 40 per cent of the workforce employed in export manufacturing.[16]

Agricultural employment is frequently seasonal and poorly paid; agricultural workers experience long periods of unemployment during which they look elsewhere for income. It is noteworthy that the trend in the formal sector, particularly in the North, is for new jobs to be increasingly part-time and held by women. In the period 1979 to 1986 two-fifths of the increase in women's employment in Canada was in part-time work.[17]

Women have problems finding employment in the formal sector, and when employed often face discriminatory practices. There is agreement that women's family and household responsibilities influence their position with the labour market. While greater educational opportunities in almost all regions have facilitated access for some women to the labour force, income inequalities persist throughout the formal sector. Many occupations in which women predominate tend to be extensions of their household and caring responsibilities; skills that are unvalued within the family are also not highly prized outside.

The myth that men are the breadwinners and that therefore women need less money is still often persistent. This is a dangerous myth, since in many cultures it affects government labour policies and government and family decisions on training and education. The gap in earnings between women and men varies considerably.

Other related factors, such as the organization of work, cultural barriers and employers' attitudes also militate against women workers' equality. Male attitudes are an obstacle too: some writers argue that men in the workplace have a personal stake in keeping women's wages low. Low wages weaken women's position in the labour market and maintain their economic dependence on men; this in turn becomes the rationale for women's ongoing responsibility for housework and liberates men for better, higher-paid and more secure jobs. Of course, the fact of having dependants to support is also a formidable constraint on men's freedom to withdraw their labour. It must also be noted that lower wage rates often make women the preferred workforce.

In some countries employment opportunities for women with little formal education remain limited because of continuing sex segregation in the labour market. For many women in Pakistan, for example, household-based production remains the main site of economic activity.

It is quite common for women outside the formal sector to be involved in multiple economic activities. Whitehead points out that in rural areas in sub-Saharan Africa:

The important but back-breaking task of planting rice is woman's work. A paddy field in India.

. . . women household members . . . may contribute to the household agricultural production or other enterprises as unremunerated family labour; in addition they may have separate access to land and other resources and may work independently, either farming or engaging in other income-producing activities.[18]

Many low-income women in urban areas also are involved in several economic activities. It is quite common for a woman to work part-time in some enterprise, take in washing, do cleaning work in houses or offices, and spend some time trading on the street.

Paid domestic work is a major area of employment for women and one for which they have the necessary skills. It is always low-paid, low-prestige and usually exploitative work which isolates women from other workers but is a ready means of earning an income. The work of domestics goes far beyond cleaning and cooking to fulfilling central roles in the employers' family life

such as child care. There are a number of long-established and successful incidences of domestic workers organizing themselves into federations or movements, particularly in Latin America and the Caribbean.[19]

One woman employing another – usually from a less advantaged social class and frequently from a different ethnic or racial background – to do domestic work that she herself cannot or will not perform remains an unresolved issue for many feminists.

DOMESTIC WORKERS AND FAMILY LIFE IN MEXICO*
Marilyn Thomson

Paid domestic work is one of the most important sources of employment for thousands of Mexican women. According to official statistics, 13.27 per cent of the female economically active population work

---

* Marilyn Thomson is completing a thesis entitled 'The Politics of Domestic Service' at the Institute of Education, University of London. This account is based on her research.

in private homes, although the number is probably much higher because of the informal nature of this type of work. Domestic work offers a certain flexibility as it allows women to enter and leave the workforce according to their family responsibilities and their life cycles and it is one of the few employment alternatives for women with little or no formal education. Domestic workers are generally among the most socially marginalized women: many are young peasant or indigenous women who migrate from rural areas to help support their impoverished families.

LA CASA HOGAR DE LA TRABAJADORA DOMESTICA

La Casa Hogar de la Trabajadora Domestica, the only one of its kind in Mexico, is a civil association and social centre which was set up by four women, three of them domestic workers, who saw the need to bring this category of workers together for mutual support. The long-term objective of the association was to try to improve women's working conditions and enable them to become aware of their rights as women and as workers.

A study of seventy-five domestic workers was carried out in the Casa Hogar over a number of years. The women represented a spectrum of personal situations ranging from single mothers to widows, but the majority were married women and common-law wives. Although all the women worked out of financial necessity, most hoped this was a temporary measure, either till they found a husband who would support them or their partner found a job. Most assumed that if their partner's employment situation improved they would no longer need to work outside their own home. According to Dora: 'When I was a young girl I never dreamed that things would turn out this way. My idea was not to have children until I was ready for them. I would get married, my

husband would support me and I wouldn't work any more; but things didn't work out that way. I don't like being a domestic, working in other people's homes, but it is the only job I could find. I want to be a mother first and foremost and wish I could spend more time with my children.'

Few of the women entered domestic work through choice. Rather, they were forced into it because of extreme poverty and their family circumstances. Another reason for working as a domestic is that in times of family crisis housing becomes a serious problem for poor single women. Of course they need to leave their children with relatives.

ATTITUDES TO MOTHERHOOD

A high number of the women interviewed attached greater importance to their role as mothers, which is permanent, than to their marital status, which was fluid. They strongly identified with motherhood which they considered to be their natural and principal role in life. Self-sacrifice was considered an integral part of a mother's role, as was testified over and over again by the women, whose own mothers had served as a role model to them. According to Rosa: 'My mother worked hard to give us an education and sometimes she would go without [food] so that we could have enough to eat. She never complained and even when she was ill she would wait on my brothers hand and foot.'

Although many of the women had very bitter experiences with the fathers of their children, nevertheless some lived in hope of finding a husband who would support them and their children financially. According to Maria: 'I want a lot of things for my children but mainly a father who loves them and doesn't hit them. I thought I could manage to bring them up to be useful citizens on my own but I've started to change my ideas about this.'

MACHISMO

Mexico is a highly patriarchal society, and traditional attitudes define the male gender role as superior to the female. The women explained how machismo had affected their family lives when they were young girls. According to Rosa: 'My brothers used to treat me quite badly. They felt superior to me because they were boys and they used to order me around. . . . My mother and I would only sit down to eat after the men had finished their meal. They didn't do anything in the house.'

A characteristic of machismo in its most extreme form is some men's lack of any sense of responsibility for their wives and children. Almost half of the women interviewed did not live with the fathers of their children, and the majority blamed male irresponsibility, in one form or another, as the main cause of their separation.

Only five women out of thirty who were not living with their children's father received any financial assistance for their children's maintenance. According to Rosa: 'Both parents should be responsible for bringing up their children but men always leave it up to us. . . . I don't want to have any more children but here in Mexico men want you to have *their* child and you've got to give them a baby or they will find another woman. If you already have children they don't think of them as their own.'

CHALLENGING THE NORM

Some of the women interviewed were beginning to question cultural values which assert male superiority and they expressed their determination not to repeat these patterns in the way they were bringing up their own children: Maria said, 'I'm going to bring up my son so that when he has girlfriends he doesn't leave children behind all over the place. If he treats a woman badly, I'll defend the woman, because I'm on the woman's side. I'm going to ensure that what happened in my family doesn't happen with my children and I want them both to know they have an obligation in the home.' ●

ORGANIZATION OF WORK AND PROTECTIVE LEGISLATION

The organization of work, particularly within the industrial sector, poses problems for women's full participation. Fixed work time and location and the separation of workplace and home can make it difficult or impossible for women to combine home and work. Such work organization, although assumed to be normal, is neither necessary nor immutable when it suits employers' interests. Improved means of communications are enabling work to be decentralized, and the growth of both subcontracting out to small enterprises and homeworking demonstrates that even the most complicated processes can be carried on away from the conventional factory floor. The need for fixed hours is also questionable given the high numbers of women part-time workers in industrialized countries. Home- and part-time workers face such drawbacks as isolation and reduced rights, but the fact remains that new ways can be found to organize work when the will is there.

Cultural norms and restrictions on relations between women and men can also seriously hamper women's employment opportunities. In societies where the sexes are strictly segregated, women require separate workplaces and dining facilities. Small employers will not willingly incur these extra costs and thus may decide not to employ women. Lack of adequate and separate transport to and from work can be a difficulty also.

Legislation prohibiting women from working at night, doing certain underground work or lifting heavy weights is increasingly being seen by women's organizations and trade unionists as a mixed blessing as it can result in discrimination against women.

Maternity leave is an essential right for all women workers. But because it is a legal

65

requirement, in some cases employers will not hire women for fear they may become pregnant. The International Labour Office (ILO) Convention on Maternity Protection (adopted in 1919 and revised in 1952) states that 'in no case shall the employers be individually liable for the cost of such benefits due to women employed by him', but in practice in many Southern countries the direct costs of the maternity leave payment, and in most countries the indirect costs of her alleged lower productivity during the pregnancy and of replacing her while on leave, fall on the employer. Local fertility rates influence the degree to which employers discriminate.

The obligatory nature of maternity leave and the prohibition on working during the leave period are under review in some countries. In 1979, the then Federal Republic of Germany and Austria introduced legislation allowing women to return to work after a compulsory minimum period; similar arrangements exist in Sweden and Finland. In Denmark, maternity leave is a right for all working women but is optional. While such respect for women's freedom of choice is laudable it could pose risks as it presupposes benevolent employers.[20]

SEXUAL HARASSMENT Sexual harassment, ranging from subtle comments and innuendo to blatant, unwanted sexual approaches and threats, is an occupational hazard for many women. Opportunities to combat this are limited; leaving the job may be the only response.

Sexual harassment is increasingly becoming the focus of women's organizations and trade union campaigns South and North. In industrialized countries, governments are adopting laws prohibiting sexual harassment, and law courts are increasingly recognizing it as a form of sex discrimination. Public and private employers are beginning to institute policies and procedures to deal with this problem in the workplace. Some Southern countries also have laws against it, and draft laws are under discussion in a number of Latin American countries.[21]

DOUBLE DISCRIMINATION Women from ethnic minorities or migrant communities face double discrimination. They are mostly employed in low-paid servicing or manufacturing work – all areas that have been hit by the recession. In the UK, for example, black women make up a high proportion of workers within the National Health Service, but predominate in the lowest-paid jobs as nursing auxiliaries or cleaning and catering workers.[22] The earnings gap between black and white women workers is decreasing slowly.

Mid-life and older women workers of all races face strong discriminatory attitudes from employers, being commonly regarded as 'past it', as no longer productive. Privatization and/or automation of production processes can lead to women losing their jobs to young men.[23]

There is clear evidence to show that the discrimination women face in entering and progressing within the formal labour market, is based entirely on the fact that they are women. Discrimination on the grounds of race and age overlays and exacerbates this fundamental abuse. This unequal treatment affects both women and their families: it is unjust to women and it denies them the opportunity to earn levels of income that could offer greater family security and well-being.

Many women workers have established their own unions, support organizations or sections within general unions to ensure their interests and priorities are addressed. Not surprisingly, women workers are interested in wages and overtime but also in health hazards, maternity leave, sexual harassment, child care and transport to and from work. The conventional union split between workplace and home issues does not match women's reality.

WOMEN-MAINTAINED HOUSEHOLDS

☐ In at least 30 per cent of all households globally women are the primary source of income. The official number of women-headed households is low in north Africa and the Middle East – 16 to 19 per cent in Egypt. In general, Asia has the lowest proportion of women-maintained households: 16 per cent. India is an exception: it is estimated that 60 million people in India live in households maintained by women, of which one-third live in extreme poverty.[25] Widowhood, husband's inability to work and desertion are among the main causes. As always, global figures hide large regional and country variations in terms of numbers, household composition and why they are maintained by women. Women who are the primary income-earners are in very many cases the *de facto*, and in some the *de jure* household head. Here, however, the term 'women-maintained' is used to describe the situation more accurately.

The concept of women-maintained households encompasses great variety: women in polygamous marriages; those divorced or deserted; women living with non-earning, low-earning or non-contributing partners; women whose partners have migrated; women migrants and refugees; widows; those who never married, with or without children; and women in unions with visiting partners.

A common feature of many households women-maintained is that either no adult male is present or if one is he contributes little or nothing to the household income. By contrast, the vast majority of male-headed households have adult women members who contribute labour, income and other forms of support.

Households maintained by women are not a new phenomenon but their numbers are increasing in many regions, and for very different reasons. A 1985 survey of metropolitan areas in Brazil, which contain about 70 per cent of the total population under eighteen years old, revealed that 96 per cent were living with their mothers.[26]

In general, rising divorce rates, enhanced life expectancy and changes in social attitudes are contributory factors everywhere which combine with specific regional situations to produce more women-maintained households. In the South, the legacy of colonization and underdevelopment has resulted in a high level of male out-migration to urban areas or abroad in search of employment, especially in sub-Saharan and southern Africa. Male migration is a significant factor in the Caribbean but perhaps more significant is the impact of slavery on family formation patterns; in recent times much family building outside marriage has been from choice.[27] The predominant factor in Latin America is economic hardship, coupled with the high numbers of consensual unions which result in women taking an overwhelming share of the burden of providing for children.

PHOTO: JENNY MATTHEWS

90-year-old Polly working in an old people's meal centre in Birmingham, UK.

War, civil strife and related human rights abuses, disappearances and persecution, for example in Central America, disrupt family units and leave women to provide for the family alone. In some Cambodian villages, aid agency workers report that women head as many as 80 per cent of households; most are widows.

High rates of divorce, separation and widowhood are the most likely causes of the rise in the number of women-maintained households in Europe and North America. There has been a noticeable increase in divorce among middle-aged women. Widowhood, too, is a significant factor elsewhere: growing numbers of households are headed by mid-life and older women, the numbers rising in direct proportion to the women's age. Men's lower longevity and the fact that in many societies the norm is for men to marry women younger than themselves account for the high number of widows.

Some women choose to become a mother and maintain their single status, and a number of women choose to live alone: these may be single, divorced, separated or involved in non-cohabiting unions. Younger women are more likely to become single parents because a consensual relationship has ended.

ECONOMIC WELL-BEING There is evidence that some women-headed households are better off in terms of general well-being, distribution of available resources and children's nutritional status; there is one less mouth to feed and the presence of a man can change spending priorities. A study of Kenyan farmers found that children in households primarily maintained by women had better nutritional status than those where a man was the main source of income.[28]

In addition to spending priorities, several other factors are significant in determining the economic well-being of women-maintained households: the woman's education and earning power, the level of financial support received from the man whether absent or not, and other family support

UP TO 30 PERCENT OF HOUSEHOLDS ARE NOW HEADED BY WOMEN. NEARLY HALF THE WOMEN HEADING HOUSEHOLDS IN DEVELOPED REGIONS AND AT LEAST A QUARTER IN OTHER REGIONS ARE ELDERLY

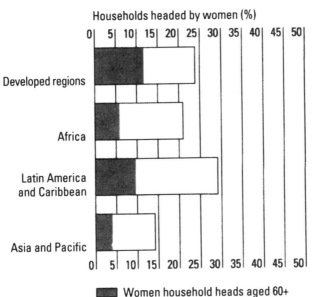

Households headed by women (%)

Women household heads aged 60+

Note: Data mainly refer to early 1980s.

Source: *The World's Women: Trends and Statistics 1970-1990*, New York, United Nations, 1991.

available from the woman's mother or other kin. In the USA, divorced women from privileged backgrounds are more likely to receive some child support from absent fathers than never-married women. In Ghana the support a woman receives from her natal family is the primary determinant of economic well-being.[29]

The evidence suggests that financially secure women-maintained households are a minority. The dependence on women as the primary source of financial support does increase the family's vulnerability. World-wide, households maintained by a woman are far more likely to have a low income than those in which a man is the primary source of support. In 1980, one out of every two households in Brazil dependent on women was at or below the poverty line; for

households dependent on a man's income the figure was one in four. Bruce reminds us that whilst women in all kinds of circumstances, including jointly maintained households, can experience poverty, it is more visible when women are alone.[30]

In contrast to the Kenyan study referred to above, one carried out by Wood in Brazil found that children born into households maintained by men had a significantly higher life expectancy than children born into women-maintained households.[31] Wood attributed this not to the fact that the woman was the primary source of income *per se*, but to the average lower income, lower educational levels, worse housing, limited access to social security and greater economic activity of those women. It is important to point out that the woman's race was one of the strongest determinants of access to resources, and of welfare indicators, such as infant mortality.

Sonnois reports that in Cambodia, too, women-maintained households are poorer: older children often are kept from school to care for younger ones and help their mothers with housework and production; health and nutrition problems are also common.[32] Furthermore, the women are too busy with daily survival to attend literacy classes or any type of educational activity.

In the USA, unmarried teenage mothers are in a particularly bad situation. They have severely limited economic resources and are likely to have less formal education, and therefore lower income-earning power, than women who delayed having children. During the early years of motherhood, nearly half have incomes below the poverty line, and of those who are unmarried and living alone with their children, almost 90 per cent were poor.[33]

In the UK, 12 per cent of all single parents, 90 per cent of whom are women, live in poverty, that is, on 50 per cent or less of the national average income. Oppenheim notes the problems that single parents face in the UK: child care facilities are few and often expensive, and part-time jobs are usually low-paid.[34] Thus many single mothers have little choice but to depend on social security payments (benefits). This situation is the focus of considerable policy debate. Bradshaw and Millar stress that there are unlikely to be 'simple or cost-free solutions' and argue for a coherent strategy that combines income support with action to enable single parents to work; this might be training, child care and other benefit arrangements.[35]

Liberating Education in New Zealand

A study of groups of solo mothers in Aotearoa/New Zealand showed that liberating education can contribute towards a lessening of these women's oppression. The groups were set up as self-help groups to bring more women out of isolation and to work with them at demythologizing their situation. Merely meeting together works at overcoming the acceptance of blame for their situation. Making it acceptable to talk to each other about their experiences validates women's experiences and counters some of the effects of isolation.

With some leadership, the women could structurally analyse their experience, which allowed them to identify the real causes of their feelings about themselves and their economic and social situation. This in turn produces more self-esteem and courage to challenge authorities and individuals who oppress them. Friendships that developed within the group meant that women could take other women with them when challenging government agencies, neighbours, and families. The sharing of information was also vital. As they became better informed about their rights, they had more solid grounds for challenging their oppressors.

Resources remain a problem. The groups were set up and run with the assistance of a government work scheme. The end of this left many groups without the resources to continue. It will take extensive numbers of solo mothers working together with other oppressed groups to bring about a fairer distribution of resources.

Elizabeth Clements, 1987 'Educating
for Change', Waikato NZ,
(unpublished MA Thesis).

AUTONOMY FOR WOMEN? Clearly, most
women have greater autonomy in households
where they are the primary financial
contributor: they have more authority to
decide on children's education, housing and
the allocation of income. This does not mean
that women are necessarily the legal household head; in certain societies men who have
divorced or deserted retain legal status as
household head. Women who in the absence
of a migrant husband become the *de facto*
head can be quickly, if temporarily, demoted
on his return.

From a purely economic point of view, a
Ghanaian woman's ideal household living
arrangement would be one that maximizes her
access to and control over resources for the
support of herself and her children.[36] Thus,
coresidence with other adults, particularly men
and most particularly spouses, gives women
greater access to land, cash income, a larger
pool of household labour, and some support
for children of whom the man is the father.

The problems facing women who are the
primary source of income in a household are
not solely economic. Single parenthood and
heavy responsibilities can bring physical
and emotional stress, loneliness and isolation.
In addition, in most cultures, if not all, being
attached to a man is a major source of social
status for women.

SINGLE PARENTS IN KOREA *
Jung-Ja Kim, Junhui Joo,
Young-ock Kim, Hae-sook Chung

In Korea between 1966 and 1980, the
number of single-parent families almost
doubled and by 1985 they represented
around 16 per cent of all families. Divorce,
separation and desertion are the main
causes, closely related to socio-economic
changes.

Two studies were carried out by the
Korean Women's Development Institute, in

1984 and 1988. Both were based on
nationwide survey results; 2,103 single
mothers and 895 single fathers were
interviewed for the 1984 study and 2,000
single mothers for the 1988 study. The
surveys were confined to single mothers or
fathers who had a least one dependent child
of eighteen years or less. Both studies
evaluated the coverage of the existing
support systems for those single parents and
included recommendations.

Almost all the single parents in the 1984
study listed financial problems as their main
concern. Although the employment rate of
single mothers was higher than that of single
fathers, and that of rural single parents was
higher than for Seoul, unstable employment
was a characteristic of the single mother's
economic activity. Many are employed on a
daily basis.

In the 1988 study, 90 per cent of single
mothers were earning a living predominantly
as domestics, farmers or factory workers.
They worked on average 59.6 hours a week,
over 6 hours more than the average for
employed women in Korea. Their average
monthly income corresponded to the income
of the lowest 20 per cent in the country,
while about 38 per cent of their monthly
expenditure went on food and beverages, 32
per cent on children's education and 10 per
cent on housing. Two-thirds of single
mothers were in debt on account of basic
expenditure on essentials. Fatherless families
accounted for 30–40 per cent of all households below the poverty line.

The emotional problems of the single
parents interviewed in the 1984 study
included feelings of hopelessness, grief and
frequent periods of depression. These
problems were more serious for single
fathers than for single mothers. About half
of the respondents had no one to consult
about personal problems and over 80 per

---

* Korean Women's Development Institute 1984 'A Study on the
Support System for Single-parent Families', and 1988, 'A Study of
the Fatherless Families in the Low-Income Group'.

cent of single mothers said they often felt angry for no particular reason. Separation or divorce frequently changed relations with the ex-partner's family and sometimes with friends.

Although single fathers had more money than mothers, they experienced more serious child-rearing difficulties, such as deterioration in school results; the number of juvenile offences committed was higher in single-father families. Single fathers received greater practical assistance from family members: in the 1984 study, only 25 per cent of the single fathers did their own household duties compared to 80 per cent of the single mothers.

Both studies concluded that the single-parent family needed a comprehensive programme of legal measures, financial support, child care, education and counselling. The 1988 report added that a more fundamental solution to the problems experienced by single parents would involve structural change: 'There is the problem of unequal distribution of wealth in society, and the unequal income structure between men and women exacerbates the problems that low-income single mothers have. It is social structural development based on the idea of equality that would provide more fundamental solutions to the problems of the fatherless families.'

The Mother–Child Welfare Act was passed in April 1989.

CONCLUSION ☐ Independent income is important to women's self-esteem and can be essential to family survival. Women's self-perception is improved by the knowledge that they are contributing financially and visibly to the household, that they are in a better negotiating position, and that should relations break down they could survive. Justice demands that women have access to all sectors and levels of employment on an equal basis with men; this requires not only legislation on equal pay and treatment but also caring support structures.

Even in this ideal scenario, however, the underlying inequality remains: independent income alone does not remove gender-based inequalities within the family or outside. At present, earning an income in almost all cases increases the number of hours women work each day.

Dwyer and Bruce, among others, argue that collective action outside is central for changing the dynamics within the household and in the wider society. In this view, instrumental to achieving this change are ' . . . extra-familial experiences which permit women an opportunity to see themselves differently, to become discomfited with their subordinated status, and empowered to confront the situation and transform the aspects of family and income relations that oppress them'.[37]

It is vital that decision-makers understand the economic relations and realities within households and adopt policies and programmes that respond to the needs and interests of each family member as well as taking measures to support the family as a unit.

1. R. Anker and C. Hein (eds.), *Sex Inequalities in Urban Employment in the Third World*, London, Macmillan, 1986, pp. 42–3.

2. D. Dwyer and J. Bruce (eds.), *A Home Divided: women and income in the Third World*, Stanford CA, Stanford University Press, 1988, pp. 2–3.

3. A. K. Sen, 'Women, technology and sexual divisions', in *Trade and Development*, study prepared for UNCTAD/INSTRAW, New York, United Nations, 1985; and A. K. Sen, 'Gender and cooperative conflicts', in I. Tinker (ed.), *Persistent Inequalities*, Oxford, Oxford University Press, 1990.

4. Sen, 1990, p. 133.

5. Dwyer and Bruce, p. 9.

6. J. Pahl, *Money and Marriage*, London, Macmillan, 1989.

7. Dwyer and Bruce.

8. S. Armstrong, 'Female circumcision: fighting a cruel tradition', *New Scientist*, 2 February 1991.

9. In J. Nash and H. Safa (eds.), *Women and Change in Latin America*, Massachusetts, Bergin and Garvey, 1986, pp. 326–43.

10. J. Hoodfar, 'Household budgeting and financial management in a lower-income Cairo neighbourhood', in Dwyer and Bruce, pp. 120–42.

11. H. Papanak and L. Schwede, 'Women are good with money: earning and managing in an Indonesian city', in Dwyer and Bruce, pp. 71-98.

12. Dwyer and Bruce, p. 5.

13. Ibid., p. 6.

14. P. Engle, 'Women-headed families in Guatemala: consequences for children', in L. A. McGowan (ed.), *The Determinants and Consequences of Female-headed Households*, Notes from Seminar Series, Population Council and the International Center for Research on Women, 1990.

15. Commission for Social Development, 'World social situation, including the elimination of all major social obstacles', Report on the World Social Situation, Thirty-first Session, Vienna, 13-22 March 1989.

16. United Nations, *The World's Women: trends and statistics 1970-1990*, New York, United Nations, 1991, p. 89.

17. International Labour Organisation, 'Situation of women workers: ILO findings', *Women at Work*, No. 2, Geneva, 1987, pp. 6-7.

18. A. Whitehead, *Wives and Mothers: female farmers in Africa*, World Employment Programme Research Working Paper, Geneva, ILO, 1990.

19. E. M. Chaney and M. Garcia Castro (eds.), *Muchachas No More: household workers in Latin America and the Caribbean*, Philadelphia, Temple University Press, 1989.

20. A. M. Brocas, A. M. Cailloux and V. Oget, *Women and Social Security: the progress towards equality of treatment*, Geneva, ILO, 1990, p. 65.

21. ILO, 1992.

22. B. Bryan, S. Dadzie and S. Scafe, *The Heart of the Race: black women's lives in Britain*, London, Virago, 1985.

23. B. Sonnois, 'Women in Cambodia: overview of the situation and suggestions for development programmes', Redd Barna, Consultant's Report, July 1990; Women Working Worldwide

(eds.), *Common Interests: women organising in global electronics*, London, Women Working Worldwide, 1991.

24. F. Hamilton, 'Association of Women Workers', in Women Working Worldwide, pp. 76-7.

25. J. Mencher, 'Female-headed/female-supported households in India', in McGowan.

26. A. M. Goldani, 'Changing Brazilian families and the consequent need for public policy', *International Social Science Journal*, No. 126, November 1990, pp. 523-37.

27. J. Massiah, 'The determinants and consequences of female headship: a Caribbean perspective', in McGowan, p. 50.

28. E. Kennedy, 'The significance of female-headed households', in McGowan.

29. C. Lloyd and A. J. Brandon, 'Women's role in the maintenance of households: poverty and gender inequality in Ghana', paper presented to a meeting of the Union of African Population Studies on 'Women, Family and Population', Ouagadougou, 24-30 April 1991, p. 8.

30. J. Bruce, 'Introduction to Seminar IV', in McGowan, p. 60.

31. C. Wood, 'Female headship and child mortality in Brazil: 1960-1980', in McGowan, p. 31.

32. Sonnois.

33. Congressional Budget Office, 1990.

34. C. Oppenheim, *Poverty: the facts*, London, Child Poverty Action Group, 1990.

35. J. Bradshaw and J. Millar, 'Lone parent families in the UK: challenges for social security policy', paper presented to the International Social Security Association Expert Group meeting on 'Changes in Family Structures and Social Security', Brussels, 18-20 September 1990.

36. Lloyd and Brandon, p. 7.

37. Dwyer and Bruce.

5 BORN TO INEQUALITY

Women, because of their sex, have essentially limited, indeed conditional, access to the 'four freedoms' which the Universal Declaration of Human Rights, and the consequent human rights covenants, aspire to define: freedom from fear and want, freedom of speech and belief.[1]

FAMILIES' INTERNAL RELATIONSHIPS and support systems and the advantages flowing to each person are complex and unique to each family unit. But it is fair to say that in relation to men there is a considerable asymmetry in the roles and responsibilities of women and in the energy, time and income they expend for the overall benefit of the family.

It is also true that women gain certain advantages from family membership, although these can be double-edged. Women are defined by the family; they have a status as someone's daughter, sister, wife or mother, but status nonetheless. Women also benefit emotionally from family life and from the support of a husband or other adults and of children. The satisfactions of loving, caring and coping and of responsibilities competently handled are great. Economic benefits can also be significant: as family members women can gain access to land and other resources and to the income of husbands or others in the family unit.

The qualification is that the family is often the sole source of status. What is conferred at the dictate or pleasure of others is never one's own autonomously; and access to resources does not mean control. Women's social status in all societies is intimately linked to and determined by the hierarchical way in which families are organized and the socially defined gender roles which are enshrined in this method of organization. Whilst patriarchal family structures and women's subordination are almost universal, each woman's social status is determined by class, race, education, economic and political circumstances; these factors result in a much higher relative status for some women than for others.

FAMILIAL INEQUALITIES: WOMEN'S SOCIAL STATUS Writing about Latin America, Jelin argues that the cohesion of the family group has had very different implications for men and for women.[2] She writes, 'For women, subordination is the result; for men, the outcome is a pattern of personal relations based on kinship solidarity, which is transferred to the public sphere of politics and productive activities.'

Other writers offer a different perspective. Writing about northwest India, Banerjee argues that the undervaluation of women's labour and other roles is both an instrument and a manifestation of the '. . . unholy alliance between social literacy, patriarchy, and diversity of group identities. . . . What the women are denied is a sense of identity distinct from the family or the community'.[3] Banerjee argues that traditionally control over women was designed to preserve social hierarchy; this preservation required the maintenance of barriers between different sections of horizontally and vertically divided social groups. In his view, this control continues today as a necessity for the maintenance of group identities in the struggle for political and economic power.

Through marriage and child-bearing, women forge alliances between families, communities, races and social groups – alliances that can be highly desirable in strengthening families and accumulating wealth, but can also conflict with the family leaders' desire to retain power over certain resources. Women, as wives and bearers of children, are so potentially subversive of the system that they must be controlled. The system, through the rules of legitimacy of children, the control of sexual access to women and men's possessional rights, as husbands or fathers or older relatives, over women, ensures that women become instruments through which the social system reproduces itself and through which systemic inequality is maintained.[4]

The institution of the family, with all its cultural accompaniments, combines with and is reinforced by state and religion to enclose women within it. Family is almost synonymous with woman and is unsurpassed in importance in most women's lives.

Women derive their sense of identity and self-worth from the family. The rewards for expertise in fulfilling the roles of wife, mother, carer, provider and household manager are few. Often the return is discrimination, and sometimes violence.

THE GIRL CHILD ☐ Advanced technology designed to diagnose genetic disorders in a foetus is now sometimes used to enable those parents who can afford it to discriminate against girls even in the womb. The results of a study of 700 pregnant women in India who received genetic amniocentesis showed that only 20 of the 450 women told they would have a daughter went through with

---

A GIRL

The air was still, the birds depressed,
the trees were like obstinate hills and
the grounds lay at rest.

The morning air was all I could breathe,
for there was someone born whom
nobody shall ever need.

The dark, small, feeble looking creature
that stepped into this world,
was brought up with the pains
she already felt,
and sorrows she had always kept.

Her inner beauty was never
attempted to be felt,
for she was disguised by
the ugliness she always held.

The time she had was cruel to her,
the life she led was unknown to her,
and the desires she possessed were
never really hers.

A forever throwaway material she was,
like a flower deprived of its freshness,
or like a fruit overbearing its staleness.

She was like a lonely beast,
unacquainted with the word 'happiness'.

Love was like an alien to her,
hostility was what she had inherited
and hatred was what she meant by life.

The helpless, innocent creature that
ought to smile, a creature that
ought to live and feel her existence,
was unaware of her purpose in life,
and had, thus, deeply resented herself
being a girl.

By: Ayesha Haroon (Karachi)
Age: 16 years

From *Subha*, the newsletter of Shirkat-
Gah, Vol. V, August 1990.

the pregnancy; all the 250 male infants predicted, even where a genetic disorder was likely, were carried to full term.[5]

It is estimated that the One Child Policy in China has resulted in the deaths of more than 1 million first-born girl infants. Two studies of parental preference in Africa and Asia also reveal that a majority prefer to have a son.[6] In many societies the social pressure on women to give birth to a boy child is intense. Failure to do so may result in violence or become grounds for desertion or divorce. The explicit disregard for a girl child is one more profound reminder to a woman of the low status of her sex.

In a culture that idolizes sons and dreads the birth of a daughter, to be born female comes perilously close to being born less than human. . . . The girl child is caught in a web of cultural practices and prejudices that divest her of her individuality and mould her into a submissive self-sacrificing daughter and wife.[7]

The situation facing most African women has been described as follows:

She is disadvantaged as soon as she is born; she is discriminated against in feeding, attention, clothing and care. . . . It has been noted that mothers give more, and more frequent, breast feeding and pay more attention to male infants. In the same vein, fathers are more interested in their male children, give more food and more attention to them. The family is ready to spend more money on male children, for clothes, schooling, health care and nutrition than on female children. Thus both parents discriminate against the female infant and child.[8]

A preference for sons is not confined to certain cultures or social classes. In many societies sons carry on the lineage and the family name, prestige and possessions, and perform religious rituals and burial rites. Discrimination against girls is not a casual or frivolous whim but the outcome of a complex combination of cultural and social attitudes and economic circumstances – the result of patriarchal and sexist social and economic relations.[9]

Most societies, to a greater or lesser degree, place a higher value on men and boys than on women and girls. This applies at every level of society: within the family; in health and care; in education and employment; and in the laws governing marriage, divorce, property ownership and inheritance. High and low values are invested respectively in the roles carried out by men and by women and affect the self-esteem and self-image of girls from birth. Added to bias is harsh economic reality: in contexts of scarcity, families make conscious or unconscious decisions to allocate their meagre resources where they will guarantee the best results – that is, to sons. Daughters can be seen as a drain on the family's resources; '. . . unfortunately for the girl child, in many cultures she is viewed as a transient to be nurtured temporarily until she marries.'[10]

The Value of Sons to Widows
Interviews with widows in rural Maharashtra, India, found that widows need not be dependent on their sons for economic security as, under both Indian and Hindu law, although only sons can inherit, a widow is entitled to use the proceeds and income from her husband's ancestral property during her lifetime. In addition, a widow directly inherits any property her husband acquired during his lifetime. However, in most cases, widows transferred property to their sons. The study also found that many of the widows who lived with their sons continued to work and were economically independent. Widows who could no longer work preferred to live with sons. Widows who lived alone or with daughters, although frequently better off financially, were less happy than those who lived with sons. Vlassoff's conclusion was that son preference is not necessarily economically motivated. Rather, sons are essential to the cultural and religious needs of the society.[11]

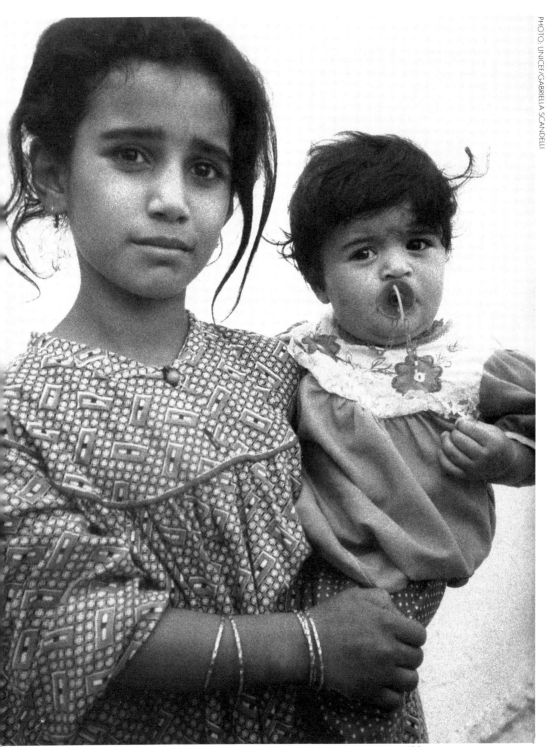

The care of younger siblings may take priority over the education of the older sister. This young girl is waiting with her brother at the health centre in Mosul, Iraq.

SOCIALIZED FOR INEQUALITY From an early age, girl children are socialized into very specific gender roles. For example, in India, 'The first lesson that a female child is made to learn . . . is that the differential treatment between her and her brothers is a fact of life.'[12] In addition, her freedom of association, communication and contact is surrounded by limits and prohibitions. She learns that the family is her sole world and that 'her vocation is the satisfaction of the immediate needs of its members' regardless of the degrees of hardship, self-sacrifice and self-effacement with which she has to cope; that her role is to mother the male family members and treat them with indulgence.

There are marked differences within regions and within countries. Agarwal points out that where women's labour participation in agriculture is low and dowry demands are high, as in northwest India, girls are more likely to be seen as economic liabilities.[13] This view is compounded by long-distance patrilocal marriages which reduce the prospect of help from married daughters. By contrast, where women's economic productivity is high or where there is a demand for female labour in agriculture, as in parts of south India, discrimination against women and girls is less prevalent.[14]

EATING LAST AND LEAST Extreme poverty and scarcity of resources can have cruel and dangerous implications for girls, but discrimination is not limited to poor families. High status gives boys priority access to the best foods and boys eat better than girls even in richer households. Ravindran found that inequity in food distribution persisted regardless of family size, income or food expenditure, implying that food availability for the family would be 'a necessary but *not* a sufficient condition' for eliminating the discrimination in food intake of female members of the family.

Differential feeding and differential care result in girls having a lower nutritional status than boys. A study of 898 villages around the world found that males were usually given priority over females in the family food distribution system. For example, a survey of families from the state of Tlaxcala in Mexico showed that girls received less of all nutrients than boys. Throughout the world, more male children are immunized and treated by hospitals than females; in a community health project in South Korea, immunization rates were equal for girls and boys when provided without a fee, but the proportion of girls fell to 25 per cent as soon as a small fee was charged.

In 30 developing countries, death rates for girls between the ages of one and four years have been found to be higher than or equal to those for boys, whereas in industrialized countries death rates for boys are generally higher than for girls. Female infants and children are generally less susceptible to infections and malnutrition than are males, due to certain biological advantages, but this trend can be reversed by external factors such as exposure to risk and the kind of care received. Worldwide, in 1991 over 125 million children between the ages of six and eleven were not enrolled in school and at least two-thirds of these were girls. Gender is the overriding constraint.[15]

From an early age the pressure on girls to assist with household work is far higher than on boys. In times of extreme economic hardship, when all family adults spend longer hours seeking and earning an income, girl children are often withdrawn from full-time education to care for their younger siblings.

It is a cruel irony that it is women who teach, practise and uphold the traditional practices surrounding differential feeding and food taboos that are so harmful to their girl children. Their own status and survival depends upon their observation and perpetuation of these customs.

VIOLENCE AGAINST WOMEN AND CHILDREN □

Men have always used violence against women to perpetuate and reinforce the gender hierarchy: to keep a woman 'in her place', to stifle her right to speak, to come and go, to make decisions and to control her sexuality. This gratuitous and persistent violence has been largely condoned by most cultures. In fact, in many cultures it was, and sometimes still is, regarded as a man's right to beat his wife, daughters, and sisters.

Abuses against women in the family have to be seen in the context of the high level of violence in general in the family: punishment of children by parents, often mild but sometimes brutal, is frequent; the link between love and violence is established and accepted. Violence is not an exclusively male phenomenon; for example, violence by women against both women and men in slavery and in colonialism, and the present-day abuse of domestic workers have been documented. Husband-battering is also a recognized phenomenon, and children and elderly relatives too can suffer cruelty at the hands of their female family or professional carers. But although not the only sufferers, girls and women are overwhelmingly the victims of violence within the family.

Young children, girls and boys, can also face physical and sexual abuse within the family in all social and racial groups, by women and men. Cases of physical battering, deprivation, and the murder of very young children appear frequently in the US and European media. Sexual abuse of children within families has always been, and remains, a closely guarded family secret. It happens most often within the child's home, involving close relatives or family friends; the abusers are predominantly men. Young girls in every society can be subjected to unwanted sexual approaches, whether tender or cruel, from men within their own family and community. Young boys too are the victims of sexual abuse. It is only within the last ten years that in some countries adult women have begun to speak out about the abuse they suffered as children. Awareness of the prevalence of incest is growing in some countries; in most, however, its existence goes unacknowledged.

Other kinds of sexual abuse of young children occur publicly: girl and boy child prostitution, abuse of street children or children sold by their parents to earn money for the family; and trafficking in young girls, accounts of which appear elsewhere.[16]

MacLeod and Saraga set out some basic steps that they see as fundamental in dealing with child abuse.[17] First, the safety of the child must be ensured immediately by removing the abuser from the home; then the child must receive emotional counselling; legal action must be taken against the abuser combined with a programme of therapy aimed 'at exploring power, anger and fear, more than sex, love and desire'.

DOMESTIC VIOLENCE Male violence has many manifestations: emotional and psychological abuse; physical and sexual abuse; and abuse of women's personal development. Physical and sexual violence by men against women in the family has to be seen in the context of the structural violence consequent upon class, gender and racial inequalities prevalent in all societies, but more extreme in some. As Mama points out:

Brutalized men are not suddenly humanized when they enter their homes to be with their families. Nor do men from the privileged classes and wealthy nations, in contexts where women are held in contempt, suddenly learn respect for women when they enter the private realm of the home.[18]

Violence against women is rarely perceived as a violation of human rights and until recently organizations concerned with the defence of human rights omitted it from their lists of violations. The extent to which

PHOTO: JENNY MATTHEWS

Violence, political or domestic, disrupts families. Women demonstrating against violence in Bogota, Colombia.

states legitimize or tolerate male violence against women in the family is often related to the levels of violence used by the state itself to survive. Authoritarian or militaristic regimes that are dependent on violence are unlikely to act to end violence against women inside their homes.

Jane Connors writes that many countries still do not regard the violence perpetuated by men against women in the home, or outside, as a serious concern:

Most [countries] refuse to penalize a husband who forces his wife to engage in unwanted sexual activity and a minority are prepared to exonerate a male relative who murders a woman who commits adultery.[19]

Rape in marriage has only recently come in some countries to be regarded as a criminal offence. Even where it has been recognized as a problem, it is rarely given high priority in terms of government action. The very term 'domestic' violence serves to minimize

the crime and conceal the identity of the abuser and the abused; responses to such violence in all societies are formed by the view that family privacy must be respected, particularly where relations between women and men are concerned.

The root causes of men's violence against women in the family are the subject of much debate, and theories abound. Whilst there is no simple explanation, its roots are closely related to the unequal power relations between women and men. Connors comes to the following conclusion:

. . . violence against wives is an outcome of the belief, fostered in all cultures, that men are superior and that the women with whom they live are their possessions to be treated as they consider appropriate.[20]

The fact that domestic violence occurs in all societies and in all social, racial, religious and age groups, although not in equal measure, would seem to support this thesis. In Mama's view:

... physical violence is just one manifestation of abusive men exercising whatever power is available to them to coerce and terrorize the women with whom they live. In other words violence occurs alongside other forms of coercion and oppression.[21]

Assault can cause severe and long-term physical damage ranging from bruising and scars to disability and death. It also has psychological repercussions. Studies cited by Connors indicate that battered women report a significantly higher level of anxiety, depression and somatic complaints.[22] Violence has the effect of beating a woman into submission and humiliating her at the immediate instance, and over a period of time of demoralizing and totally undermining her self-esteem, thereby making it increasingly difficult for her to take action.

Rathbone-McCuan suggests that if an older woman had lived with an abusing spouse for many years the pattern may have become normative; older women may more willingly accept domination by a husband; and those who are financially and emotionally dependent on a husband may be unaware of alternatives or reject them, fearing loneliness and insecurity.[23] Older women too are less likely to report cases of spouse abuse and seek assistance.

Family violence also affects young children, who may be physically and psychologically hurt. Connors writes that: '. . . there is fairly clear evidence that observation or experience of violence in family of origin may be implicated in later violent behaviour unconnected with the home.'[24]

LEGAL RESPONSES Current thinking is that domestic violence should be criminalized as a separate offence as has happened, for example, in some Australian states and elsewhere. There are disadvantages associated with criminalization: the abused woman may be unwilling to testify against her partner and may be forced to choose between imprisonment for contempt and testifying in court. It is possible for discretion to be used by the judge in these cases. There are other problems too, as pointed out by the critics of the 1990 Law for the Prevention of Domestic Violence passed by the Puerto Rican government, namely: prison overcrowding; the judicial system may not be prepared for the many cases presented; and the scope of the definition of the offences.[25]

Connors sets out a number of guidelines for the legal system:

- **Police must develop adequate protocols and act to eliminate the existing ambiguities and gaps in law that deprive women of adequate legal recourse.**

- **Women must have assured access to legal remedies should they wish to use them.**

- **The attitudes towards wife assault of those involved in the law must be scrutinized.**[26]

Connors calls for an integrated and co-ordinated service linking the police, medical, social welfare, health and women's refuge services, a service which addresses both the short-term and the long-term needs of the woman and her children. She warns about adopting a rigid approach which may result in further victimization. In her view flexibility of response is essential, as each woman is different.

It is clear that what is required is a holistic response to violence against women, one which includes counselling services for the abuser as well as for the abused. Safe refuge houses enable women and their children to leave a violent situation with the knowledge

81

that there is somewhere secure and welcoming to go to. Refuges exist in many countries but rarely in adequate numbers or with sufficient funding to meet the need. Community or religious groups and social services can play a key role both in working to counter violence and in supporting the abused woman. Several countries have launched national education programmes to raise the issue as a subject for public discussion, to give it prominence and, as a consequence, to change attitudes.

EDUCATING AGAINST VIOLENCE IN PAPUA NEW GUINEA AND AUSTRALIA

Not all women who are assaulted by their men can resort to the police and leave home. In Papua New Guinea most rural women who are victims of violence feel it is better to stay than to leave. If a woman leaves, in the long term she often has no option but to return; relatives probably will not have her back as this would necessitate repaying the brideprice and giving her land on which to grow food. Another major deterrent is that leaving her husband usually means leaving her children too because in patrilineal societies the children belong to the father.

The Law Reform Commission therefor, decided to concentrate on changing people's attitudes through a nationwide campaign of posters, leaflets, radio programmes, children's books and a video. The village courts, the police, the churches, schools and women's groups were the targets of the campaign. The campaign deliberately adopted a conservative, family-oriented approach, as any direct mention of women's rights would have allowed people to dismiss the programme as a 'foreign feminist idea'. Although it is difficult to assess the actual reduction in levels of violence without further research, the awareness work certainly has made people talk and think about the issue for the first time.[27]

In Australia, the National Domestic Violence Education Program run in the period 1987–1990 aimed to raise awareness of domestic violence as an issue of

WIFE-BEATING IS WRONG BECAUSE:

- It is against PNG's Laws
- It is against PNG's Constitution
- It is against our Christian beliefs
- It spoils our family life
- It is a bad example for our children
- It can cause serious injury or death

There is a leaflet with more information about the law on wife-beating. You can get it at the police station, District Court, welfare office, Public Solicitor's Office, Aidpost or Health Centre.

Women and Law Committee, P.O. Box 3439 Boroko. Tel: 30 0722

community concern, provide accurate information, encourage widespread community participation in the campaign, and change attitudes.

An element of the programme was a National Domestic Violence Month organized to highlight the issue with local and national activities. Information kits, posters and pamphlets were prepared with specific videos, booklets and radio programmes for Aboriginal and Torres Strait Island women, immigrant women, young women and those living in isolated rural areas. The month was launched by the Prime Minister, thus testifying to government commitment to tackling the problem of domestic violence.[28]

The Latin American and Caribbean Network against Sexual and Domestic Violence is a network of women working in non-governmental organizations as well as individual women with a feminist perspective who work independently in this area. Its objectives are:

- to continue to provide an opportunity for exchange of information about work and experiences;

- to deepen and connect the work of institutions, organizations and women's groups in order to create national networks;

- to make contact with public and private national institutions in order to get the problem of violence onto their respective agendas;

- to develop the power to negotiate from a position of autonomy.

The Network is co-ordinated by Isis International, Santiago, Chile.

SOURCE: ISIS INTERNATIONAL, *WOMEN IN ACTION,* ISSUE 3-4, 1990

TRADITIONAL PRACTICES ☐ In all cultures at some stage women have been subjected to practices that derive from tradition, custom or religious belief. Many of these practices still prevail in some societies; all are harmful, some are violent, some can result in a woman's death.

The payment of dowries from the bride's family to the groom's is problematic for the woman and for her family. In India, the size of dowry demands has risen astronomically in recent years. The harassment of the woman at the hands of her husband, his mother or other in-laws in order to extract more dowry can start from the moment she arrives in the house of her husband's family. In extreme cases, if she fails to deliver the money she is eventually murdered.[29] Deaths related to dowry received only minimal public attention and appeared to be of no interest to politicians until the late 1970s, when women's groups in the bigger Indian cities began to organize protests, publicize the deaths and demand justice. Despite this, the number of dowry deaths rose sharply from 1980.

Of all traditional practices, female genital mutilation has attracted most, and not always helpful, international attention. The practice is common in the Horn of Africa, through to west Africa, the Middle East, in parts of South-east Asia and in Asia in several religious groups. It can include the removal of all or part of the clitoris and the labia minor, and/or stitching together the two sides of the vulva. The age of the child subjected to this practice varies from a few days old to adolescence; it is also known to be practised shortly before marriage and, in some cases, after the woman has had one or two children. It is widely believed that this practice has less to do with initiation into womanhood and more to do with the wish to control female sexuality and conserve the monogamous status of women. The practice has many specific objectives, including the desire to preserve virginity, and therefore the marriageability of young girls; the desire to protect women against their own sexuality and limit that sexuality; and the desire to protect family lineage in order to ensure stability of the family unit.

Female genital mutilation destroys a crucial zone of sexual pleasure. Whatever its origin and purpose, the health risks associated with it are undisputed. These include immediate complications of haemorrhage, infections such as septicaemia and tetanus, increased vulnerability to contracting HIV, damage to adjacent organs, and violent pain – any of which could cause collapse or sudden death. The longer-term complications are: keloid scarring; chronic infections, which may lead to infertility; menstrual problems; gynaecological and obstetrical complications; and immeasurable psycho-logical damage.

Those who regard this practice as harmful and want to work towards its eradication have advocated or adopted a number of responses: education; legal prohibition; and measures to protect the child's rights.

- Education: Berhane Ras-Work, President of the Inter-African Committee on Traditional Practices Affecting the Health of Women and Children (IAC) calls for the eradication of female genital mutilation and other harmful practices by the year 2000. The IAC set up national committees in 22 African countries. Their main activities include special training and information campaigns for opinion leaders, and training or orientation of traditional birth attendants (TBAs) and other practitioners.

- Legislation: Legal prohibition of the practice plays an important part in combating this problem. A combination of legislation and well-designed information and education measures could help greatly to abolish the practice.

- Female genital mutilation as child abuse: This view of the practice has gained international support in the form of the United Nations Convention on the Rights of the Child. This approach is highly controversial and is opposed by, among others, the London Black Women's Health Action Project, who say that they do not want 'these families to be alienated and labelled as child abusers, therefore criminals.'

Legislation, health education and campaigning on children's rights are all key elements, but one or other may be more appropriate in any given time, community and country. Once again, measures that improve women's status are fundamental to the permanent removal of all harmful practices.

STATUS WITH AGE? ☐ Women in some societies experience a marked improvement in their social position as they grow older. Studies from Corsica and the Lebanon showed that older women became 'confident grandmothers and assertive household organizers'. In addition, they and others considered that they aged more successfully than men. Women in some Muslim societies experience far fewer constraints on their behaviour and mobility as they grow older, having successfully fulfilled the ideal of mothering and nurturing. However, such power as women gain is always limited by economic dependence on men.[30]

The transition to old age is not always trouble-free: dislocation from work and home, reduction in income, restrictions on social roles, bereavement and, in some cases, rejection, abuse or neglect accompany old age.

Despite the fact that elderly women have spent their lives caring for others, many live in adverse conditions, enduring the combined effects of ageing and sexism with the cumulative effects of limited opportunities and resources.[31]

In most countries, advancing years are no guarantee of enhanced status. A study carried out in Delhi found that more older women than men considered that their status within the family had deteriorated with age, primarily as a result of widowhood and financial dependence.[32] They also claimed that city life was undermining the traditional respect expected from daughters-in-law. The situation in Kenya is similar:

To be old in Kenya used to be the best part of life. The elderly were respected for their great age and wisdom, and played important roles in society as judges, teachers and community leaders. With the advent of Western education and Western values, the knowledge

possessed by the elderly is now less useful and they consequently play a less central and less respected role in the community. In addition, the elderly are often left behind in the rural areas when the young people migrate to the cities in search of employment. Less than ten per cent of the elderly receive pensions, and women rarely qualify for any pension at all.[33]

In the USA and in other Northern countries, the fact that some older women, and men, suffer actual abuse at the hands of their carers is slowly gaining recognition. It is estimated that the vast majority of such cases never reach the public's attention, and that with the increase in longevity in these countries the problem will likewise increase.

CONCLUSION □ Where women's lives have been exclusively defined by their capacity to bear children, becoming a mother, especially of a son, can substantially improve their lives and status. But once this capacity passes, women's position can become uncertain and vulnerable. It is only through acquiring an individual identity that this dependent status can be removed and with it discrimination against girls.

The low social status of women and the consequent power imbalances between women and men are the underlying reasons for harmful and discriminatory practices and physical and sexual violence against girls and women in all societies. The responsibility for this injustice and violence lies not only with the immediate family but also with each community, religious organizations, health and social service professionals and law enforcers, where they exist. In the final analysis what is required is change at the deep level of gender relations. Mama writes thus:

... it has become clear that changing the material inequalities must be part of a wider project to change the cultural, social and emotional inequalities that also characterize relations between the sexes.[34]

1. G. Ashworth, *Of Violence and Violation*, London, Change, 1985.
2. E. Jelin (ed.), *Women and Social Change in Latin America*, London, Zed Books, 1990, p. 2.
3. N. Banerjee, 'Family postures vs family reality: strategies for survival and mobility', *Samya Shakti*, Vol. IV and V, 1989–90, pp. 210–19.
4. Meeting on Women and Violence, January 1985, Surat, India, cited in G. Kelkar, 'Violence against women: an understanding of responsibility', in M. Davies (ed.), *Third World, Second Sex 2*, London, Zed Books, 1987.
5. S. Ravindram, 'Health implications of sex discrimination in childhood', WHO/UNICEF unpublished paper, 1986.
6. UNICEF, *The Girl Child: an investment in the future*, New York, 1990, p. 14.
7. Department of Women and Child Development, *The Lesser Child: the girl in India*, Ministry of Human Resource Development, Government of India, 1991.
8. Inter-African Committee on Traditional Practices Affecting the Health of Women and Children (IAC), Report of the Regional Conference held in Addis Ababa, 19–24 November 1990.
9. M. Mies, *Patriarchy and Accumulation on a World Scale*, London, Zed Books, 1986, p. 153.
10. UNICEF, p. 15.
11. Carol Vlassoff, 'The value of sons in an Indian village: how widows see it', *Population Studies*, No. 44, 1990.
12. M. Mukhopadhyay, *Silver Shackles: women and development in India*, Oxford, Oxfam, 1984, pp. 11–12.

13. B. Agarwal (ed.), *Structures of Patriarchy: the state, the community and the household*, New Delhi and London, Kali for Women and Zed Books, 1988, p. 3.
14. Ravindran, p. 3.
15. UNICEF, p. 23.
16. Isis WICCE, 'Poverty and prostitution', *Women's World*, No. 24, Winter 1990/91.
17. M. MacLeod and E. Saraga, 'Challenging the orthodoxy: towards a feminist theory and practice', *Feminist Review*, No. 28, pp. 16–55.
18. A. Mama, *The Hidden Struggle: statutory and voluntary sector responses to violence against black women in the home*, London, London Race and Housing Research Unit, 1989, p. 300.
19. J. Connors, *Manual on Violence against Women in the Family in Commonwealth Countries*, London, Commonwealth Secretariat, 1992, p. 3.
20. Ibid., p. 12.
21. Mama, p. 300.
22. Connors.
23. E. Rathbone-McCuan, 'The abused older woman', in G. L. Caravaglia (ed.), *The World of the Older Woman: conflicts and resolutions*, New York, Human Science Press, 1984, pp. 53–6.
24. Connors, p. 11.
25. M. Gonzales-Baez, 'Legislating against violence in Puerto Rico', *CAFRA News*, Vol. 4, No. 3, September/November 1990.
26. Connors, p. 42.
27. C. Bradley, 'How can we help rural beaten wives? Some suggestions from Papua New Guinea', paper presented to the

Welsh Women's International Conference, 1988.
28. Connors, pp. 43-4.
29. Mies, p. 147.
30. M. J. Storey Gibson, *Older Women around the World*, Washington, International Federation on Ageing in cooperation with the American Association of Retired Persons, 1985, p. 11.
31. F.L. Paltiel, 'Women and mental health: a post-Nairobi perspective', *World Health Statistics Quarterly*, Vol. 40, No. 3, 1987, pp. 233-66.
32. Storey Gibson, p. 13.
33. *AgeAction*, No. 2, 1990-91, published by HelpAge International.
34. Mama, p. 303.

EXTERNAL
INFLUENCES

The inequality of women in most countries stems to a very large extent from mass poverty . . . caused by underdevelopment, which is a product of imperialism, colonialism, neo-colonialism, apartheid, racism, racial discrimination and of unjust international economic relations. The unfavourable status of women is aggravated in many countries, developed and underdeveloped, by *de facto* discrimination on the grounds of sex.

Women, by virtue of their gender, experience discrimination in terms of denial of equal access to the power structure that controls society and determines development issues and peace initiatives. Additional differences, such as race, colour, ethnicity, may have even more serious implications in some countries, since such factors can be used as justification for compound discrimination.[1]

THE FAMILY UNIT, its formation patterns, structures and functions are shaped by a range of external forces. Religion and culture are two direct and significant influences on the family and on the position of women within it. The early Christian missionaries actively imposed their views on family matters on other cultures, as do some of the evangelical missionaries today. Slavery and colonization, and their legacy of under-development have had profound effects on social organization. The eighteenth, nine-teenth and twentieth centuries brought new influences, both benign and detrimental. The economic development programmes implemented by governments were, and are, founded on certain ideals of family life and women's and men's responsibilities within it.

RELIGION AND CULTURE ☐ Religion and culture are closely linked and play a central role in shaping the value system and the norms of social organization in most societies, often influencing state legislation, for example on divorce or contraception, or overriding it in importance to the individual in cases where the law is more liberal. All major religions revere the family as the basic social unit and the natural framework in which children and adults receive the material, emotional and moral support they need for their well-being and development. Thus they believe the family unit must be respected and strengthened, and it is in this context that women's position is defined within marriage and the family. Women are the anchor of the family and their duties as mothers and wives should override all other concerns.

Most major religions see women in a secondary position in relation to men, although the implications of this vary widely from one religion to another. As women are also commonly regarded as a potential source of social and moral disorder, most religions subscribe in some degree to the view that women and their behaviour require careful regulating. There is an inconsistency in the Christian view of women, which is present also in other religions: on the one hand women are perceived as temptresses and weak, on the other as pure and selfless madonnas. Caldwell writes that in real life women are put in an impossible position: '. . . sanctity, as the condition for motherhood, can only be gained humanly by forgoing the other condition of sanctity, virginity.'[2]

Some Christian churches which previously endorsed the subjugation of women to men within the family have now altered their thinking to the view that relations between women and men should be based on complementarity and mutuality. Such changes are reflected, for example, in the modern marriage rites. Many, however, remain traditional in their approach.

Hinduism, though quite egalitarian in earlier times, appears to have regressed to regard women as inferior to men and to endorse pre-puberty marriages for girls.[3] Although Buddhism is described as a gentle and egalitarian religion, men are regarded as superior and women as secondary. About Thailand, Somswasdi writes:

Being born a woman is generally believed in this Buddhist country to derive from sin committed in her previous life; only men can be ordained; significantly, a woman will gain merit through her son entering the monkhood. Before getting married, a man is usually urged by his mother to be ordained first, so she would not have to share the merit with his wife. Women can only be good Buddhists by supporting the religion but cannot gain merit by entering the monkhood.[4]

Islamic teaching, as currently interpreted, is equally clear on women's status: 'Men have the authority over women because Allah has made the one superior to the other, and because they spend their wealth to maintain them. Good women are obedient' (Sura 4:34). Benjelloun notes that clear roles are laid down for husbands and wives: 'As head of the family, his wife must obey him except when he goes against sacred laws; he is there to educate and advise her; offspring from the marriage carry his name.' The wife has the right to a dowry and 'to be treated fairly and with respect, and the right to be provided for (in every meaning of the word).[5]

Confucianism prescribed the lowest positions socially and legally for women, who were often held in contempt.[6] Confucianism laid down the 'three cardinal guides': ruler guides subject, father guides son, and husband guides wife. For women there were the 'three obediences': to father before marriage, to husband after marriage and to son after the death of the husband; and 'four virtues': morality, proper speech, modest manner and diligent work.[7]

What is officially pronounced on religion and what is preached within each community and practised within each family varies. In many religions, women researchers and groups are working to reinterpret religious texts or reform religious practices. Researchers studying the history of Islam have found that in the first Muslim society women had much more independence.[8] Historical events and different interpretations of the Koran have brought about changes.

The secondary status of women is one of the true universals, a pan-cultural fact. Yet within that universal fact, the specific cultural conceptions and symbolizations of women are extraordinarily diverse and even mutually contradictory. Further, the actual treatment of women and their relative power and contribution vary enormously from culture to culture, and over different periods in the history of particular cultural traditions.[9]

In most societies, women are the primary transmitters of culture: language, knowledge, music, traditions, rituals, remedies, recipes, and behavioural patterns – all of which are central to each person's sense of identity. A society's culture is not a static package, and the definition of its essential elements varies from time to time reflecting current power structures and influences. Mukhopadhyay writes that an essential part of the socialization of girls is to give them the responsibility of transmitting ritualistic behaviour: 'This ensures that in the observance of the norms of socio-religious behaviour women will

Women play an important role in cultural activities. Bangalore, India.

remain the pillars which uphold those traditions which often resist the changes necessary for development.'[10]

Societies and cultures under threat or domination, for example, due to invasion, civil strife or large-scale migration, are vigorous in the protection of their cultural traditions. The cultural imperialism of Western mass media is regarded by many states as a great menace to their traditions. The ways of life of the Maori, Aborigines and the indigenous Indian populations in North, South and Central America were marginalized and demeaned by colonialism, but are still vibrant today although excluded from national cultural life. Ethnic minorities, both immigrants and their descendants living in countries where another culture dominates, are not any different in this respect. An understanding of the history of slavery and African culture is central to the consciousness of black women living in

Britain or in other Northern countries: 'Our African origin is the cornerstone of our lifestyle and our perception of the world, the internal dynamic which has enabled us continuously to resist new assaults on our way of life.'[11]

Culture is not gender-neutral; some of its components can be discriminatory and harmful to women, as we have seen above. Frene Ginwala, of the African National Congress Women's League, speaking at a conference in 1990 stressed the importance of making a clear distinction between cultural practices 'which provide social cohesion for communities and those which harm people. We must protect positive practices and outlaw harmful ones.' Each woman's status is deeply rooted, shaped, and intertwined with the culture of the society in which she lives.

Cultural conservation can be a mixed blessing for women. According to Warnock, the conflict with Israel and its effective denial of the existence of Palestine has led Palestinians to attach crucial importance to an idea of their national cultural heritage in which the family and women's traditional roles within it are central.[12] Recent years have seen a more rigorous enforcement of seclusion and the wearing of the veil or scarf by women in public. Some writers argue that the age-old antagonism between Islam and Christendom created 'an area of cultural resistance around women and family' which together came to represent 'the ultimate and inviolable repository of Muslim identity'.[13]

The second half of the twentieth century witnessed the development of so-called mass culture promoted through improved telecommunications and transport. Widespread access to mass media, and television in particular, has exposed people everywhere to the fast and flashy lives of soap opera characters which have come to be synonymous, incorrectly, with 'Western lifestyles'. The rise in fundamentalist tendencies in many religions which has marked recent decades is not unconnected with the all-pervasiveness of mass culture. Evangelical movements are currently vociferous in some Christian churches, in Hinduism, in Islam and other religions. All such movements adopt a conservative stance in relation to women which usually has negative implications both for women's rights and for equality within the family.

THE DEVELOPMENT PROCESS □ The kind of economic change that took place in Europe in the eighteenth century and from there spread west, east and south in the following two centuries is characterized by industrialization, the mechanization of agriculture and mining, and the emergence of market economics. These changes led eventually and inevitably to the accumulation of wealth in fewer and fewer hands, local and foreign. The colonial legacy combined with the new economic format to

WOMEN LIVING UNDER MUSLIM LAWS

This is a network of women whose lives are shaped, conditioned or governed by laws, both written and unwritten, drawn from interpretations of the Koran tied up with local traditions.

The objectives are:
- to create links amongst women and women's groups (including those prevented from organizing or facing repression if they attempt to do so) within Muslim countries and communities;
- to increase women's knowledge about both their common and diverse situation in various contexts;
- to strengthen their struggles and to create the means to support them internationally from within the Muslim world and outside.

In each of these countries till now women have been waging their struggle in isolation.

For women in Muslim countries/communities the aims are:
- providing information for women and women's groups;
- disseminating this information to other Muslim women;
- supporting their struggles from within and making them known outside;
- providing a channel of communication.

These objectives are fulfilled through:
- building a network of information and solidarity;
- disseminating information through 'dossiers';
- facilitating interaction and contact between women from Muslim countries/communities, and between them and progressive and feminist groups at large;
- facilitating exchanges of women from one geographical area to another in the Muslim world.

SOURCE: INTERNATIONAL SOLIDARITY NETWORK, FRANCE

ensure a bias in favour of growing cash crops for export to the detriment of food production for local consumption, and, in Africa, to the detriment of women farmers.

The rise of factory-based mass production, whether in Chicago, Colombo or San Salvador, brought new and different jobs, initially mainly for men. This work, organized separately from home and family production and reproduction, reinforced the existing gendered divisions of labour. In the South, the process of industrialization was shaped by the colonial and neo-colonial relationship: the raw materials and products from the newly independent states would continue to fuel the economies of the North. Economic interdependence was entrenched.

The late twentieth century advances in technology and telecommunications, controlled by a handful of Northern-based corporations, dominate current economic developments worldwide and further cement interdependence. The new international division of labour that has been created is very like the old colonial one and still firmly based on the same gender and race lines.[14] The advent of telecommunications and the mass media, again dominated by the North, means that almost every individual, family, society and culture is exposed to outside influence; outside influence has ambiguous effects on social organization.

FALSE ASSUMPTIONS Most social and economic programmes in Southern countries in the second half of the twentieth century, whether funded by external or by internal finance, have had as their underlying premise a certain family model. This assumed a one-couple nuclear household with an income-earning husband as head, a non-income-earning wife and their children. This single false assumption not only undermined the capacity of the programmes to achieve their stated objectives but had lasting detrimental implications for women and children.

Since the 1950s, social and economic improvement, or development, has been seen by both the external and internal planners solely as a problem of economics. By producing more, exporting more and earning more foreign currency, 'developing' countries would 'develop', and in turn this wealth could be used to invest in social programmes. Women and children featured only as assumed beneficiaries of the greater wealth that would accrue to men. When the indicators showed that this strategy was not bringing about improvements in the living standards of the majority, other programmes were added which aimed at meeting families' 'basic needs' for food, shelter, water supplies, health care and sanitation. Women were to be the channels of these basic needs; but still the multiplicity of women's roles remained unseen. Women's needs, and by inference family needs, were assumed but not investigated.[15]

When the indicators failed to show that poverty had been defeated, further programmes were added to enable women to earn some income to meet their own and their families' needs; this income continued to be perceived as supplementary to that of the assumed male breadwinner. There followed a plethora of small-scale income-generating projects, initiated and funded by the development agencies, which were always marginal to the mainstream modern economy and failed to address women's needs for the new skills required by that economy. In addition, they did nothing to improve women's status or to arm them to challenge the structures which perpetuated the inequalities they faced. In reality, the projects reinforced gender inequalities, were time-consuming and generated little income.

During the United Nations Decade for Women, 1976-85, a new strategy for integrating women in the process of development (known as Women in Development, WID) was adopted by the development organizations. Special components were added on to agricultural programmes for example, whereby women farmers would have access to extension training, credit facilities and sometimes land. The strategy had three problems. First, as many writers have pointed out, women have always been integrated in development and usually on unequal terms; thus the problem is not 'insufficient or inadequate participation' but rather 'their enforced and asymmetric participation in it, by which they bore the costs but were excluded from the benefits'.[16] Second, women's existing roles and responsibilities were ignored; and third, as has been pointed out by Sen and Grown and others,[17] the WID strategy failed to question the model of development on offer and seemed to take for granted the inequalities in international and national economic structures and thereby to assist in reinforcing them.

A development action that contributed towards increasing inequalities for women and children involved land settlement schemes associated with agricultural programmes; one such was the Accelerated Mahaweli Development Programme, a major irrigation and resettlement scheme in Sri Lanka. No account was taken of the fact that women are responsible for growing food crops such as pulses, maize, manioc and vegetables; they were perceived as dependent housewives.[18]

In the early years of the Mahaweli Programme land was allocated only to male heads of households, aside from those women who already owned land. Poor women were denied access to the new assets – land, credit, training, extension services and marketing information – and were excluded from participation in decision-making. They were relegated to unpaid family labour or wage labour,[19] and given half-acre compounds around the houses, barely enough for a latrine and some fruit trees.

Special legislation for the scheme laid

down that only one heir, usually a son, could be appointed, in order to pre-empt fragmentation of land holdings. This was contrary to the traditional Sinhalese inheritance rules which prescribe that sons and daughters inherit equal shares of paddy land, cattle and other properties.[20] This change in property relations between men and women, however, was not accompanied by a change in men's obligations towards family maintenance: research showed that only 35 per cent of male farmers' net incomes (after debts were paid off) benefited the rest of the household.[21]

An evaluation of rural development projects financed by the European Development Fund in eight African countries in the four sectors of rural development – rain-fed and irrigated agriculture, animal husbandry, forestry, and village drinking water supply – found that in only two of the nine projects did women participate and benefit to a fairly high degree.[22] It also found that women did not automatically benefit from development interventions and that where they did not constitute an explicit target group, projects often had the unintended negative effect of increasing women's workload without offering any countervailing benefits. By contrast:

Projects or components which did involve women as a target group often reduced their workload and improved their income by enabling them to obtain land, credit, animal traction, extension advice, inputs and marketing services.

This is not to say that all economic and social programmes in all countries since the 1950s failed to achieve their objectives. Many programmes in agriculture, education, community health care and water supply were successful in increasing farmers' incomes, in opening new opportunities and in directly improving social conditions for women, men and children. Smaller-scale programmes started by local non-govern-

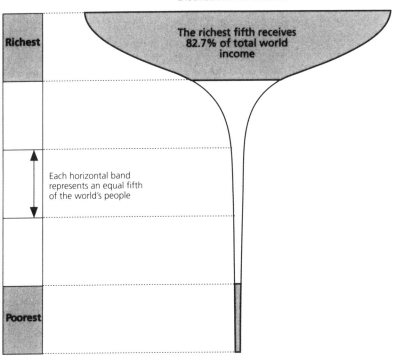

WORLD POPULATION ARRANGED BY INCOME

Distribution of income

Richest

The richest fifth receives
82.7% of total world
income

Each horizontal band
represents an equal fifth
of the world's people

Poorest

The poorest fifth receives
1.4% of total world income

World population		World income
Richest	20%	82.7%
Second	20%	11.7%
Third	20%	2.3%
Fourth	20%	1.9%
Poorest	20%	1.4%

Source: UNDP, *Human Development Report 1992*, New York, Oxford University Press, 1992.

mental organizations (frequently funded by North-based NGOs) have often been more rigorous in responding to the specific needs and interests of women and incorporating gender-planning ideals and techniques. Nevertheless, in Jayaweera's view:

In an economic environment in which more and more women are pushed into long hours of employment to meet family needs, and in a context of gender relations which promote inequitable allocation of resources, labour and time within the family, women's workload has increased without adequate returns for their labour inputs. . . . External interventions that support women in their multiple roles have been minimal. Very little has been done to empower women to control the resources they generate and to counter patriarchal social relations that dominate both family life and economic and social relations of production.[23]

POLICIES ARE CHANGING: PRACTICE TAKES A LITTLE LONGER In response to criticism from strong women's lobbies inside and outside the multilateral and bilateral organizations, and faced with the harsh facts of failed development initiatives, food insecurity, and growing rural and urban poverty, the international community began to review the situation and a recognition of women's central place in social and economic life emerged; some international agencies have adopted gender policies and incorporated gender planning into their staff training programmes. There is some room for doubt that in all cases the inspiration is a commitment to women's rights *per se*. It cannot be overlooked that this recognition runs alongside, and also runs counter to, the commitment of the international financial institutions to structural adjustment programmes and to the privatization of public services.

SOME POLICY STATEMENTS

In 1985, UNICEF reaffirmed 'its commitment to strengthen support actions that will yield direct social, health and economic benefits to women living in poverty, for their own well-being and in recognition of the fact that improvement of women's condition is a necessary prerequisite for the improvement of the health and well-being of children'.

Since then, UNICEF has developed 'a programme strategy that will strengthen the links between socio-economic development programmes directed to women at the household level and the child survival and development strategy, recognizing the inter-dependence between the health of children and the availability of resources to enable women to care for their children, as well as the benefit of reduced illness and improved child health and welfare to the mother and family'. UNICEF 1985. See also *Implementation Strategy for UNICEF's Policy on Women and Development*, 1987

'FAO's Plan of Action for the Integration of Women in Development is dedicated to enhancing women's participation through projects and programmes that systematically bring women into the mainstream of development initiatives and national life. Within this framework, future activities will give greater recognition to women's special needs for income-producing activities and control of income, education and training opportunities, and technologies and other means to ease the burden and increase the productivity of women's work.'

Food and Agriculture Organization, *Women in Agricultural Development: FAO Plan of Action, 1990*

'IFAD's policy is not to address "women in development" in general or simply in social terms but to promote the economic empowerment of poor rural women.'

Idriss Jazairy, International Fund for Agricultural Development IFAD March 1991

The old development model remains largely intact but the environmental crisis is highlighting its shortcomings and calling some of its basic tenets into question. 'Sustainable development' is now the aim, and women are seen to be 'instrumental' in this. The recent pronouncements on human resource development reflect a view of women, and men, not as active agents in the development and conservation process but as resources to be 'harnessed' for production and reproduction.[24]

The fact that to a great extent development has been conceived exclusively in economic or income-earning terms has had serious repercussions for women and the family, because much family-related work is carried on unpaid and outside the market place. Many researchers and activists are calling for a rethink of the concept of development strategy. Elson outlines this view:

The starting point is that any development strategy should be centrally concerned with reproduction as well as production, and with the way these activities are articulated with one another. The entitlements of those having prime responsibility for care of other family members need strengthening. This means not so much more opportunities for women to undertake more work; but more resources under the control of women. This will have a long-term pay-off for national development objectives, not just through increasing productivity but also through its impact on fertility.[25]

ECONOMIC CRISIS AND RECESSION □

The global situation in the last decade of the twentieth century is characterized by extreme poverty for almost 500 million people, declining standards of living for the majority, and extraordinary wealth for the minority. As women and the economic crisis is dealt with fully in a companion volume to

HUMAN RIGHT TO DEVELOPMENT

The concept of a human right to development comes as a rejection of the kind of development practised to date and emphasizes:

- human development, that is, putting people first;
- equity;
- respect for social and cultural values;
- respect for ecology;
- participation as both a means and an end;
- economic growth with a human face;
- progressive realization of *all* the human rights of *all*.[26]

this one,[27] this section will concentrate on the direct implications for women and the family.

The international economy in the 1980s was marked by sharp rises in real interest rates, the ensuing debt crisis, and the measures recommended by the international financial institutions to deal with the situation. Since the early 1980s new loans to the debtor countries are given under certain conditions defined by the International Monetary Fund (IMF) and the World Bank; these conditions are packaged within structural adjustment programmes (SAPs) designed first, to achieve a balance of payments equilibrium in two to five years, and second to stimulate economic recovery. Without an IMF-type SAP or similar, debtor countries were and are deemed ineligible for new credit; this 'conditionality' is also applied to certain kinds of aid.

IMPACT ON FAMILY SURVIVAL Women were and are adversely affected by the economic crisis and the SAPs across the full range of their lives and work. The Commonwealth Expert Group on Women and Structural Adjustment wrote:

Women are at the epicentre of the crisis and bear the brunt of the adjustment efforts: it is women who have been most severely affected by the

deteriorating balance between incomes and prices, and who have desperately sought means for their families to survive. It is women who had to find extra work to supplement family income . . . who have rearranged family budgets, switching to cheaper foods, economizing on fuel, and disposing of consumer durables, wherever possible. It is women who have organized and participated in efforts to counter the crisis by communal buying and cooking; and it is women who have been most immediately affected by cuts in health and educational facilities, and by the rising morbidity and deaths among their children. Women . . . have had the greatest responsibility for adjusting their lives to ensure survival.[28]

Currency devaluations caused sharp falls in real wages, while inflation and the removal of subsidies pushed up the cost of food and other basic commodities. Together with the introduction of charges for health care and education, the result was dramatic declines in household incomes and living standards.

UNICEF's study of the impact of structural adjustment policies confirms that deteriorating health and nutrition are widespread and that standards of education and health services are also declining in many countries. UNICEF found that in many Southern countries during the 1980s malnutrition increased, infant mortality rates rose again after decades of decline, and the trend towards improvement has been halted. Diseases thought to have disappeared, like yellow fever in Ghana and malaria in Peru, have reappeared. Education has also been affected: in Chile and Ghana primary school attendance fell and drop-out rates rose; child labour has become more common. In Sri Lanka there is evidence that literacy and school attendance decreased from 1979 to 1981.

The reduction in public services and privatization displaced women who were generally well represented in public sector employment. Industrial workers were also adversely affected because, following trading liberalization, domestic industries could not compete with cheaper imports from abroad. New opportunities for employment, such as in the private sector, were insufficient to offset declines elsewhere.

SAPs aimed to increase agricultural productivity but paid no heed to the situation of women farmers, to the fact that women and men grow different crops, to obligations on women to provide labour on husbands' fields, to women's restricted land rights, or to their limited access to the cash economy, farming inputs, technology and training. Ingrid Palmer points out that the premiss that land productivity can be increased for internal use or export by relying on higher-yielding crops and chemicals is based on the implicit assumption that 'more labour time can be squeezed out of women for the more labour-intensive practices which result from these increases in land productivity'.[29]

It has been suggested by a number of writers that the combined effect of declining living standards, increases in infant mortality rates in some countries, the near demolition of public health services and demands for increased labour power within the family, could be that women, and men, would decide to have more children.[30] It has also been suggested that the increasing stress associated with making ends meet has exacerbated violence against women.

Antrobus and others are clear that the structural adjustment package was founded on women's capacity to cope, to replace the cuts in services, to work longer and harder, and to put their own needs and interests aside in favour of those of their families.[31]

The economic recession in many Northern countries has had many of the same repercussions on people's lives, although the impact is not so severe. The cost of living has risen at the same time as unemployment. There is growing poverty in many Northern countries and increasing differentials between the very rich and the very poor. These

PHOTO: JENNY MATTHEWS

This drop-in centre in Brazil offers support and guidance for street girls and their children.

inequalities were present even in the so-called boom years but inevitably became more extreme in times of recession. One effect of the recession was that several Northern countries adopted a much more cautious approach to spending on social security, child care facilities and community support organizations.

In the USA, the world's largest debtor country, two out of every three adults at or below the poverty level are women. Nine million children receive no routine medical care, and 1 in 20 women receives no prenatal care at all or none until the last three months of pregnancy. Poverty rates are higher amongst black, Hispanic and other ethnic minority groups: nearly 50 per cent of black children live in poverty, and they are twice as likely as white children to have no regular source of health care and more likely to be seriously ill when they see a doctor.

It is too soon to quantify the total long-term damage suffered by the majority of women, men and children in the South as a direct result of the debt crisis and structural adjustment measures. It seems likely that the trends already prominent in Southern countries must be exacerbated: migration, urbanization, impoverishment of rural areas, all of which lead to the dispersal of family units and the separation of family members for short or long periods of time. For very low- or no-income families in the North, too, the implications are harsh. It is clear now that the social costs of aiming to achieve economic stability and recovery in Southern countries within a five-year period were too high.

HUMANIZING ADJUSTMENT Whilst it is widely accepted that economic adjustment is necessary, what is not agreed is its nature, scope and extent. UNICEF has promoted the concept of 'adjustment with a human face', that is, 'the conscious adoption of policies which protect the well-being of the vulnerable during adjustment, both in the short and medium term'.[32] The international financial institutions retain their commitment to structural adjustment, but now include measures to protect some public spending to mitigate the worst social impact.

Others, including many NGOs, argue for an adjustment or development strategy which includes the Northern countries, and also addresses political and social structures.

The immediate reality is that for many millions of women the multiplicity of responsibilities that families and societies place on their shoulders have become increasingly impossible to fulfil in a satisfactory or even in an adequate manner. There is also a longer-term significance: the limited progress made towards equality for women in the areas of education, training, employment and health care has been reversed and undermined.

UPROOTED FAMILIES □ There are currently over 20 million refugees in the world, 80 per cent of whom are women and their dependent children. These refugees are located in over ninety countries worldwide. In addition, it is estimated that there are over 25 million people displaced within their own countries. The causes are legion.

Persecution or the threat of it is not the only reason people flee their homes: famine and economic hardship have caused whole communities to move in search of relief. It is estimated that there could be a dramatic increase in the numbers of refugees and displaced people in the next twenty to thirty years in consequence of environmental degradation. Yet another cause is some governments' forcible resettlement of peoples within their own country. In the last twenty years the South African government removed millions of black people from their traditional homes to new so-called 'homelands'. These internal exiles live in conditions as harsh as in any refugee camp but have not qualified for any refugee assistance.[33]

PHOTO: WORLD COUNCIL OF CHURCHES/PETER WILLIAMS

In times of grief, other family members may be an important source of strength. A Nicaraguan family mourning 19-year-old soldier killed in a Contra attack.

Families inevitably suffer when people are forced into exile. Parents become separated from children and family members may find themselves on different sides of a border. Single people, too, are affected by separation from their relatives and community. Leaving home with little warning or preparation, under threat of military conflict or famine, is a horrifying and traumatic experience. Life in most temporary settlement camps is uncomfortable and unpleasant, and becomes unbearable when stays are extended indefinitely. For many refugees the situation is exacerbated by grief at the death of a child or other relatives and uncertainty about the well-being of absent family members. Tensions mount due to anxiety, scarce resources, fear of the future and close proximity with and dependence on others.[34]

Leaving home is particularly difficult for older people, who may find it physically difficult to leave war-torn or famine areas and make the journey to safety. Furthermore, in times of scarcity, the elderly are likely to receive low priority in the allocation of food, health care and training.[35]

PRINCIPLE OF THE UNITY OF THE FAMILY
The United Nations High Commission for Refugees (UNHCR) has sought since its inception to reunify separated family members. UNHCR encourages governments to adopt broad and flexible criteria of family reunification, such as liberal admission policies and flexibility in expecting documentary proof of marriage and the filiation of children. In order to promote the rapid integration of refugee families in the country of settlement, it is UNHCR's view that 'joining close family members should in principle be granted the same legal status

FRAMEWORK FOR ASSISTANCE TO FAMILIES

Elizabeth Ferris has identified the following four elements which assist in developing a family-oriented strategy of assistance:[36]

- Programmes established to meet the basic needs of uprooted people should be designed with the family in mind and with a good understanding of family structures in each particular community;
- Particular attention must be paid to the roles of women within the household or family. Women-headed households are common. In order to earn an income, women need day care centres where children can be left securely;
- Women's own personal needs must be considered, in addition to addressing needs associated with family roles;
- A family-oriented strategy should include educational, psychological and vocational counselling.

and facilities as the head of the family who has been formally recognized as a refugee'.[37] Strict immigration regulations in many countries, Europe and the USA for example, make family reunification extremely difficult.

In exile, family roles change. Women, the majority in most camps, may find themselves, as heads of households, undertaking activities that are new to them. In the refugee camps on the Algerian border, where 160,000 Sahrawis have spent over 15 years, women who make up three-quarters of the adult population have played a central role in running the camps from the time of their arrival. They set up committees for health, education, local production, social affairs and provisions distribution.[38] Similarly, Guatemalan women refugees who settled in Mexico during the 1980s to escape the civil war and human rights abuses back home have changed from quiet rural Indians to political activists. While in exile the women launched literacy campaigns and small businesses and became highly organized and politicized. These new skills will be much needed for rebuilding their communities when their exile ends, but undoubtedly they may lead to conflict with neighbouring communities who stayed in Guatemala and retained more traditional attitudes.[39]

Men also have to come to terms with changes in their position: they are often forced into idleness which undermines their status and traditional authority.[40] Over a period of time frustration may lead to violence directed at women and children.[41]

When women try to take the lead, the possibility of future social change opens up, but it can also lead to conflict. Brazeau points out two potential problems: a woman may face difficulties in readjusting to her home country if that society has maintained the traditional social structures and division of labour in her absence; and in some societies, the shortage of men resulting from conflict may force women into polygamous or very early marriages for economic reasons.

RESETTLEMENT Returning home, the preferred option of the vast majority of refugees, may be stressful for individuals and families. The parents' expectations may not be met on return and these expectations may not be shared by children returning to a homeland they have probably not seen before.[42] For those who cannot return home but instead settle elsewhere, adjusting to a new country with a different culture, language, food and physical environment as well as values can be extremely difficult. It is easier for children and adolescents for whom, as Hardy points out, 'cultural adaptation can be something of an adventure';[43] this in itself can lead to tensions between old and young as 'younger refugees tend to deliberately discard aspects of their parents' culture'. Resettled families can face racially motivated hostility from the local people in the new country.

Adapting to resettlement can be particularly hard for women. They may face isolation, and find it impossible to obtain employment, or learn the new language. Men also face equally difficult obstacles: their skills and qualifications may be unrecognized or unusable, while the social status and self-esteem they enjoyed at home may be reduced by unemployment or less demanding jobs.

Resettlement countries have different attitudes about how newcomers should behave. Often these countries do not allocate any or adequate resources to enable newcomers to have the facilities they need to maintain their cultural identity.[44]

INDIVIDUAL STATUS The universal refugee definition contained in the 1951 Convention and its 1967 Protocol does not include gender as one of the grounds for persecution that will lead to refugee status being granted. Women who face particularly severe gender-based discrimination may be considered a 'particular social group' within the 1951 definition and gain eligibility this way but not as individuals. This lack of individual documentation places women in great danger.

The problems faced by refugee women are similar, if not identical, to those faced by women generally in their countries of origin and asylum with the added anguish and complications following flight.[45]

A DETERIORATING ENVIRONMENT □ Concern for the environment is growing daily with ominous pronouncements about our deteriorating atmosphere and degradation of natural resources. The consequences of the mismanagement of resources, including deforestation, soil erosion and pollution, are especially harsh for women and children. Davidson writes that it is clear that women's long-term environment interests have been damaged by inappropriate development.[46]

ORGANIZING AS CONSUMERS

In June 1965, in an attempt to combat rising prices, one housewife from Tokyo's Setagaya district organized 200 women to buy 300 bottles of milk. From this one bulk purchase, the Seikatsu Club was formed in 1968.

The club buys around 400 basic products in bulk, mainly food but also some clothing and kitchen utensils, and delivers them directly to its membership of over 150,000, 80 per cent of whom are women. It is financed by each member contributing an initial investment of 1,000 yen to join the cooperative. This is returned if the member leaves. They refuse to handle products such as synthetic detergents which are detrimental to the health of the members or the environment; they work directly with local farmers to ensure food is organic.

The club has a democratic structure and is committed to empower each member with a voice and role in participatory politics. Since 1979, club members have taken a more active role in local politics. Under the slogan 'political reform from the kitchen' 33 members have been successful in municipal elections.

Collectives offer housewives an opportunity to work to their full potential. The labour of most Japanese women is wasted on unskilled, part-time work. But through managing their own businesses, members not only reap job satisfaction, they are able to make a constructive contribution to their local communities.[48]

All day long, I lie asleep under the thorn tree, and the desert is on this side of me and on that side. I have no work to do. We are all waiting for the rain, as we cannot plough without rain. I think the rain has gone away again like last year . . .

Tomorrow the sun will rise, quietly. The many birds in the bush will welcome it. I do not. Alone, without the help of rain it is cruel, killing and killing. All day long we look on it, like on death.

Then, at evening, all is as gentle as we are. Mother roasts goat meat over the coals of the wood fire. Sister feeds her baby. Grandfather and cousin Lebenah talk quietly to each other about little things. The stars spread across the sky and bend down at the horizon. The quiet talk of grandfather and cousin Lebenah seem to make earth and heaven come together. I do not know what we would do if we all did not love one another, because tomorrow the sun will rise again.[47]

> As food producers, fuel and water gatherers, women are the main natural resource managers in large areas of the South.

Women depend on natural systems - soil, water, forests - for their own and their families' survival and frequently for their livelihoods. They are often totally dependent upon 'free' goods such as fuel wood and fodder which they collect from 'common property' environments. For women, improved health, incomes, status and self-esteem can all come from natural resources; therefore they have a vested interest in environmental protection and repair.[49]

> But women are frequently excluded from development planning and environment conservation decision-making.

Any new strategies for the proper pursuit of developmental and environmental concerns . . . ought not to be worked out by the 'experts' and only commended to the poor rural women for implementation. They ought to go beyond the cosmetic 'involvement' of a select few among women - which carefully co-opts the vocal elites. The new strategies must provide a platform from which village women themselves can articulate their proposals for solutions. It is now high time they too got an audience![50]

> While sustainable development is on the international agenda, many women are sceptical about the international community's commitment to change:

I would like to ask whose common future we are talking about when we talk about the urgency of saving the resources of this planet for the future. Can we really have a programme for 'sustainable development' as a common concern without unpacking this term 'development', without looking at the way this term is predicated on the notion of the Western model of development. . . . By talking about common futures are we in danger of subsuming the interests of the less powerful by the dominant concerns of the more powerful?[51]

CONCLUSION □ Within each society, religion and culture combine as the fundamental influence on the formation and structure of the family and relations within it. Modern economic development has overlaid and reinforced this foundation. Neither influence is gender-neutral nor entirely beneficial to the advancement of women. Women everywhere are analysing the elements of these influences from a gender perspective.

A gendered perspective is essential when assessing the implications of economic changes and environmental degradation on women and their families, and in determining the way forward. Redclift suggests that such a perspective would involve an examination of gender differences and similarities in four key areas: rights over the environment, energy systems, reproductive control, and knowledge systems. She writes:

A 'regenerative' approach to development would need to put these issues at the centre. We cannot create sustainability on the basis of existing gender inequities, because to do so is once again to subsume women's interests under the notion of general and, in this case, even global well-being.[52]

Measures to strengthen women's political, economic and social rights are essential to environmental conservation and sustainable economies. Some other specific points emerge:

- An early resolution to the debt crisis is critical for the well-being of millions of families;

- There is an urgent need to devise a concept of development that is concerned with reproduction as well as production and that is applied to the North as well as to the South;

- Women refugees must be granted individual status and their specific needs recognized and addressed.

1. 'Forward-looking Strategies for the Advancement of Women', adopted by the World Conference to Review and Appraise the Achievements of the United Nations Decade for Women, 1985, paragraphs 44 and 46.

2. L. Caldwell, *Italian Family Matters: women, politics and legal reform*, London, Macmillan, 1991, pp. 19–20.

3. *Balai*, Vol. II, No. 4, December 1987.

4. V. Somswasdi, 'Women in the Constitution of Thailand: a far-fetched hope for equality', in *Women's Legal Position in Thailand*, Chaingmai University, Women's Studies Programme, Faculty of Social Sciences, May 1991, pp. 1–19.

5. M. A. M. Benjelloun, 'The family in the Arabian culture', paper presented to the international conference 'Families and Cultures', Paris, UNESCO, 4–5 December 1987.

6. *Balai*, Vol. II, No. 4, December 1987.

7. Wei Zhangling, 'The family and family research in contemporary China', *International Social Science Journal*, No. 126, November 1990.

8. L. Ahmed, 'Women and the advent of Islam', in *Women Living under Muslim Laws Dossier 7/8*, Grabels, France 1989–90.

9. S. Ortner, 'Is female to male as nature is to culture?', 1974, cited in H. L. Moore, *Feminism and Anthropology*, Cambridge, UK, Polity Press, 1988.

10. M. Mukhopadhyay, *Silver Shackles: women and development in India*, Oxford, Oxfam, 1984, p. 12.

11. B. Bryan, S. Dadzie and S. Scafe, *The Heart of the Race: black women's lives in Britain*, London, Virago, 1985, p. 183.

12. K. Warnock, *Land Before Honour: Palestinian Women in the Occupied Territories*, London, Macmillan, 1990, p. 52.

13. D. Kandiyoti, (ed.), *Women, Islam and the State*, London, Macmillan, 1991, p. 7.

14. S. Mitter, *Common Fate, Common Bond: women in the global economy*, London, Pluto Press, 1986.

15. H. Allison, G. Ashworth and N. Redclift (eds.), *Hard Cash: man-made development and its consequences, a feminist perspective on aid*, London, Change and War on Want, 1986.

16. V. Shiva, *Staying Alive: women, ecology and development*, New Delhi and London, Kali for Women and Zed Books, 1988, p. 2.

17. G. Sen and C. Grown, *Development Crisis and Alternative Visions: Third World women's perspectives*, New Delhi, DAWN, 1985.

18. S. Jayaweera, 'Women and economic equality', paper prepared for the Third Meeting of the Commonwealth Ministers Responsible for Women's Affairs, Ottawa, Canada, 9–12 October 1990, p. 13.

19. Ibid., p. 14.

20. J. Schrijvers, 'Blueprint for undernutrition', *Sociologia Ruralis*, 24, 1984, pp. 255–73, cited in D. Versteylen-Leyzer, 'La participation des femmes au developpement', *Revue du Marché Commun*, No. 319, July/August 1988, pp. 383–8.

21. Versteylen-Leyzer.

22. D. Versteylen-Leyzer, 'Integrating women in development: the experience of nine European Development Fund rural development projects', *Courier*, No. 125, January/February 1991, pp. 14–18.

23. Jayaweera, pp. 15–16.

24. F.L. Paltiel, 'Education to identity and solidarity', in Report of the Fourth International Working Seminar 'The Caring Society in a Threatened Society', 11–15 July 1990, Institute for Study in Salzburg, pp. 41–50.

25. D. Elson, 'Gender Issues in Development Strategies', paper presented to the seminar on Women in Development, Vienna, 9–11 December 1991.

26. Clarance J. Dias, 'Law and the development process within the Asia Pacific reality', in Asia Pacific Forum on Women, Law and Development (ed.), *My Rights, Who Control?*, 1990, pp. 1–17.

27. J. Vickers, *Women and the World Economic Crisis*, London, Zed Books, 1991.

28. Commonwealth Expert Group on Women and Structural Adjustment, *Engendering Adjustment for the 1990s*, London, Commonwealth Secretariat, 1989.

29. I. Palmer, 'Gender issues in structural adjustment of sub-Saharan African agriculture and some demographic implications', ILO World Employment Programme Research Working Paper, Geneva, ILO, 1988, p. 3.

30. Ibid.

31. P. Antrobus, 'Strategies for change: design of programmes/plans', paper for the Commonwealth Caribbean Regional Meeting on Structural Adjustment, Economic Change and Women, 1990.

32. UNICEF, *The State of the World's Children*, Oxford, Oxford University Press, 1987.

33. L. Ngcobo, 'Forced to leave: forced migration of South African women', *African Woman*, No. 3, Spring 1989, pp. 9–10.

34. United Nations Centre for Social Development and Humanitarian Affairs, Draft Report of the Expert Group Meeting on Refugee and Displaced Women and Children, Vienna, 2–6 July 1990.

35. K. Tout, 'The ageing dimension in refugee policy: perspectives from developing nations', *Ageing International*, Vol. XVI, No. 1, June 1990, pp. 6–10.

36. E. Ferris, 'A world turned upside down', *Refugees*, No. 70, November 1989, pp. 20–22.

37. United Nations High Commission for Refugees, Conclusion No. 24 (XXXVII) of the Executive Committee on the Reunification of Separated Refugee Families, 1981.

38. War on Want, *Women for a Change*, campaigning pack, London, War on Want, 1987.

39. M. Talbot, 'So near and yet so far: Guatemalan refugees wonder is it safe to return', *Newsweek*, April 1992, p. 20.

40. Tout.

41. C. Brazeau, 'Gender sensitive development planning in the refugee context', paper presented to the Expert Group on Refugee and Displaced Women and Children, July 1990.

42. Ferris.

43. L. Hardy, 'Relative values', *Refugees*, No. 70, November 1989, pp. 35-6.

44. Ibid., p. 36.

45. See S. Forbes Martin, *Refugee Women* (London, Zed Books, 1992), for an in-depth examination of women refugees; see also United Nations High Commission for Refugees, Note on Refugee Women and International Protection, submitted to the sub-committee on international protection at the Forty-first Session of the Executive Committee of the High Commission Programme, 28 August 1990.

46. J. Davidson, 'Background discussion paper', in *Focus on the Future: women and environment*, Report of the OECD's Development Assistance Committee Expert Group on Women in Development Seminar, Paris, May 1988, London, IIED, p. 34. For a more detailed examination of the issues see A. Rodda, *Women and Environment*, London, Zed Books, 1991.

47. B. Head, *Tales of Tenderness and Power*, Oxford, Heinemann, 1990.

48. S. Maruyama, 'Seikatsu: Japanese housewives organize', in C. and J. Plant, *Green Business: hope or hoax?*, Hartland, UK, Green Books, 1991, pp. 80-82.

49. J. Davidson, 'Women and the environment', paper prepared for the Third Meeting of the Commonwealth Ministers Responsible for Women's Affairs, Ottawa, Canada, 9-12 October 1990.

50. S. Nyoni, 'Women, environment and development in Zimbabwe', in the Report of the Women, Environment and Development Seminar, 7 March 1989, Women's Environmental Network and War on Want, p. 27.

51. M. Mukhopadhyay, 'Women's struggle to save the forest in India', in *Women and Sustainable Development*, Report of the Women's Forum, Bergen, Norway, 14-15 May 1990, London, IIED, 1990, p. 8.

52. N. Redclift, 'Developing a gendered perspective on sustainable development', unpublished notes, 1991.

BUILDING EQUALITY IN FAMILIES

violates the principles of equality of rights and respect for human dignity, is an obstacle to the participation of women, on equal terms with men, in the political, social, economic and cultural life of their countries, hampers the growth and prosperity of society and the family and makes more difficult the full development of the potentialities of women in the service of their countries and of humanity.

Human rights for women is the collective right of a woman to be seen and accepted as a person with the capacity to decide or act on her own behalf and to have equal access to resources and equitable social, economic and political support to develop her full potential, exercise her right as a full human being and to support the development of others.[1]

AN ESSENTIAL FIRST STEP to building equality in the family is to remove gender-based discrimination against women. Equal opportunities for women and men are fully compatible with the protection and support of families. This compatibility can be seen in several policy areas, for example, a shorter working day and week, parental leave, equal opportunities in training, and equal rights in social security.

The Convention on the Elimination of all Forms of Discrimination Against Women was adopted and opened for signature, ratification and accession by the United Nations General Assembly on 18 December 1979. It entered into force on 3 September 1981; by September 1991, 104 countries had ratified the convention, many with reservations. Significantly, more reservations were lodged against this (over eighty) than against any other United Nations Convention.

The starting point of the Women's Convention is discrimination:

> ... extensive discrimination against women continues to exist ... [this]

The convention lists a range of measures which the States Parties should adopt, for example, in education, public life, nationality rights, employment, health care and in their constitutions and laws to eliminate discrimination against women. It stipulates that women and men should have the same rights to enter into marriage and to choose a spouse, the same rights and responsibilities during marriage, at its dissolution, and as parents, irrespective of their marital status, in matters relating to their children (Article 16).

Even when ratified, the implementation of the convention remains at the discretion of each party state; ratifying states do, however, commit themselves to regular reporting to the Committee on the Elimination of All Forms of Discrimination Against Women (CEDAW) which meets annually to consider progress. International covenants such as the Women's Convention, are important in setting and defining international standards, and the reporting process is an incentive to action. They do not in themselves alter the harsh realities of life.

LEGAL EQUALITY Before and since the convention, and mainly in response to pressure from women's organizations, many governments amended their countries' constitutions to enshrine equality between women and men. The motives were both ideological and pragmatic.

Legal equality is important: it validates women's struggles for equal rights and access to resources and makes equality a public issue. Of course, constitutional changes alone cannot end patriarchy or overturn centuries of discrimination. The speed at which the road from constitutional reform to real equality is travelled depends primarily on the political willingness of each government to reorient its priorities towards ending discrimination and creating a more equitable and just society. Even when the will to act exists, it can be severely hampered by budgetary crises and a hostile international climate. Governments less committed to women's rights are all too ready to give macro constraints as an excuse for inaction.

Constitutional equality can leave the real foundations of discrimination untouched. The vast body of laws in each country which regulate business, employment, social security, property, marriage, divorce and inheritance can impinge on women's rights. In Peru, the Political Constitution of 1979 and the 1984 Civil Code provide for full equality, but other laws and codes, such as those on minimum marriage age and property management in marriage, are still discriminatory.[2]

In Thailand, the 1974 Constitution contains an equal rights provision but the 1976 Family Law discriminates against women in many respects.[3] A man, if abiding by his traditional culture, may still give property to a woman's family in return for her agreeing to marry. A man may enter a claim for divorce on the ground of the woman's adultery, but not a woman, unless her husband has given maintenance to or honoured another woman as his wife. Furthermore, the Thai state closes its eyes to the sexual exploitation of thousands of its women and young girls.

Even when the laws are progressive, other factors can prevent women exercising their rights. Kelkar[4] writes that although India's constitution has declared sex equality a guiding principle, in practice, the subordination of women to men and junior to senior pervades family life in all classes and castes. Inheritance is just one example: daughters often waive their land rights in favour of their brothers; widows, too, tend to surrender their inheritance rights to their sons to avoid being denounced as selfish and becoming alienated from their family. (See Chapter 5.)

Many governments have raised the legal age at which women and men can marry either as part of a process of social reforms designed to enhance women's position in the family and outside or to increase their participation in the formal economy. It is also used as a means to reduce the birth rate. The link between education and marriage age has been documented. In Sri Lanka, for example, in order to increase women's participation in the labour force the government put more resources into women's education. As a result the literacy rate rose to 70 per cent for women, and over 80 per cent of women under twenty years old were unmarried although the legal age for marriage remained twelve years. Of course, education alone cannot guarantee equality or equal treatment in employment.

Although countries that underwent a socialist-inspired revolution, such as China, Cuba, North Korea, South Yemen or Nicaragua, granted formal equal rights to women, some writers question the commitment to women's equality and suggest it was largely motivated by political considerations. Molyneux argues that while the more extreme inequalities were removed, conditions for full sexual equality were not secured because this was not the primary aim of the reforms. She claims that the main objective was to remove the old order by attacking male supremacy over women, precapitalist property relations, the patriarchal family and religious orthodoxy, and to reconstruct a stable social order based on a 'formally egalitarian, preferably nuclear, family'. As the danger of counter-revolution receded, women gradually ceased to be defined as militant revolutionary agents:

They are represented instead as both wage workers and mothers, as both the physical and social reproducers of the next generation and as those with primary responsibility for educating and nurturing the young.[5]

This is not to deny that in many cases serious and practical steps have been taken to enable women to command the resources necessary for equality. In Nicaragua, for example, under the Sandinista government a number of important measures aimed at removing gender inequality were implemented, in the areas of sex education, child care, literacy, training and employment; sexist advertising was also banned.

Constitutional and legal changes, however progressive, do not make it possible for women to assume their rights. A further commitment is needed to public education to inform women and men of the legal situation and to change attitudes towards women. The state, the legal profession and women's organizations have key roles to play in changing attitudes.

GAINING AN IDENTITY □ For women a strong sense of identity and self-esteem are crucial for creating new gender relations both within and outside the family. However, centuries of subordination and subservience cannot be removed rapidly or without struggle. Identity and sense of self-worth are shaped by many factors: education and income; the availability of natal and conjugal family support; and the level of sexual, class and racial discrimination each woman experiences.

There is a growing consensus that participation in collective organizing actions outside the family and the home is a key step towards gender equality. However, women's particular place in the family structure and socially defined gender roles limit the forms of public action many women can take. In most societies women are responsible for relations between families while men are responsible for relations between communities.

Most women experience three specific gender constraints: multiple roles and responsibilities; the sexual division of labour; and the fear or actual experience of sexual or physical violence. Jelin adds that the ideological burden of being female hinders women's public participation.[6] Most women have very little time to devote to formal political activities. Even when they find or make time they frequently feel disaffected by male-dominated bureaucratic structures which rarely give priority to issues of relevance to women. Men's opposition to women's equal participation in *their* structures also cannot be ignored.

Nevertheless, women have always played key roles in their communities even if they were not described or perceived as leaders. In recent decades many women have emerged as community leaders, either because men have left the community or because they wanted to ensure that the women's views were heard. Women have also played key roles in labour disputes, in *ad hoc* defence committees, and human rights and national liberation struggles. Their actions and participation have not always been recorded in history, neither have women been guaranteed a place in national-level decision-making.

In low-income rural and urban communities as well as among the middle classes, more formalized women's organizations are a growing phenomenon. These range from peasant women's confederations to credit unions, community health councils, human rights organizations and political movements. Some take a more conventional family welfare approach; others have a political agenda; they specifically set out to empower, to challenge the status quo, and they start from an analysis of their own situation. Each in a different way can increase consciousness and enhance confidence.

PHOTO: UNICEF/SEAN SPRAGUE

Some men are beginning to realize how important it is to share family responsibilities, such as caring for children. A young family in Rajshahi district, Bangladesh.

SHAPING THE NATIONAL AND INTERNATIONAL AGENDA In countries where revolutionary political change took place in the second half of the twentieth century, mass movements were established to mobilize each sector in the process of reconstruction and transformation. Initially imposed from the top, some in time went a long way to develop grassroots participation and began to set their own agenda, for example the National Association of Nicaraguan Women (AMNLAE), and the National Union of Eritrean Women (NUEW). During the 1980s under the Sandinista regime, AMNLAE broadened its role from speaking on behalf of women in the capital to building real support throughout the country. Despite the externally backed Contra war, local consultations were set up to discuss priorities and demands, and strong alliances were created with trade unions, such as the Association of Agricultural Workers, to ensure that at every level of society women were gaining practical equality. The NUEW had a leading role in shaping social reforms in Eritrea (see Chapter 2).

In many countries feminist organizations are gathering strength at national level and challenging institutionalized discrimination in education, employment and in state structures. Their primary objective is the democratization of society in all spheres of human activity, beginning with gender relations.[7] These organizations have played a key role in gaining public and political acknowledgement for issues hitherto ignored, such as women's multiple responsibilities, reproductive rights, the sexual division of labour, and physical and sexual violence against women.

Women's political parties are still a rarity, but women have set up groupings within existing parties to raise their voices from a position of collective strength. Slowly, they are making a dent in that great bastion of men's power, national politics. In the 1985 general elections in Peru two women stood as independent candidates in loose alliance with the United Left. They adopted the slogan 'Women vote for yourselves' and raised issues around women's workload, sexuality and violence never before mentioned in an election debate. Although not elected, they did achieve a high public profile.

It is impossible to do justice to the numbers and scope of women's organizations. They focus on issues ranging from day-to-day survival strategies to visionary programmes for alternative development policies based on gender equality. It is noteworthy but not surprising that in the first instance most women organize for the benefit of their family. Only when their consciousness is raised about their own situation do they begin to question and challenge gender-based inequalities. Gradually, through this process women gain some sense of a separate identity. Some concept of explicit needs and interests distinct from those of their family is central to this discrete identity. A highly desirable parallel process would be the closer integration of men's needs and interests with that of their families.

SOCIAL POLICY ☐ Through its social policy, each state can, if it chooses, play an important role in enabling women and men to fulfil their family responsibilities while at the same time eliminating gender-based inequalities. Social policy can, of

FROM MOTHERS TO DAUGHTERS
Sanna Naidoo

Here,
our children were born,
Here we women,
Refusing to be defeated,
disillusioned,
sang, hoped, sorrowed . . .
Believing
That the norms,
taboos . . . our society imposed . . .
contrived . . .

Together
We can now, dispel . . .
Changing a system
That continued
To steal . . .
Minds . . . Hearts
Bodies . . . egos.
- our aspirations
- our identities . . .

And Rise
Challenging new limits
New possibilities . . .
To illuminate lives . . .
expanding
Horizons . . .
To go up for ever,   .
From Here . .
From mothers
To daughters . . .
From woman
To woman
Colouring lives anew . . .
Refusing to be
Children . . .
Refusing to be
Put into Places . . .
By those
who claim
to be our Superiors
- our keepers

Source: *Agenda*, No. 9, p. 34.

course, also reinforce and exacerbate existing inequities.

A state's policy on family matters is rarely encapsulated in one document; it is reflected in the wide range of legislation in such areas as maternity and parental leave, social security, rights, property and taxation. Legislation on education, health, employment, housing and transport also accurately mirrors a state's perspective on the role of the family in the society and on gender roles within it. Views alter over time as a result of changing social attitudes, economic circumstances and fertility rates as well as political priorities. This section looks at some of the components and related policy issues central to women and the family.

The ideal family policy should cover everything affecting the family's emotional, educational, economic and social role, that is, everything relevant to 'people living in families'. It should seek to strengthen the collective unit and to improve families' living conditions, and thus make it easier for them to have and bring up children. Family policy must recognize diversity in family forms. In the view of the Confederation of Family Organizations in the European Community (COFACE) a clear distinction must be drawn between family policy and demographic policy:

A policy with purely demographic aims could pose a threat to families' dignity and right to make their own decisions. A true family policy . . . could have a positive impact on demographic evolution.[8]

The arena of family policy is surrounded by controversy. There are those who argue that the state has intervened too much in family affairs, and has thus usurped parental rights and responsibilities and diminished family solidarity and internal support systems. But even before the modern state, patronage, religious or other institutions provided some support for families. Family solidarity is a valuable and central part of family life, but

may need external support. Others argue the problem is not state intervention as such but the exclusion of parents from the process:

In many cases, this [state] support is an obvious necessity, but parents have participated very little. In some cases, they have been kept in the background or even excluded with the result that parents have lost interest in some aspects of the development of their children, or have been overwhelmed by a feeling of frustration resulting in demobilization.[9]

Few women or men want the state to take over raising their children but most need social services to enable them to maintain their family responsibilities. In both the South and the North, the hostile economic climate and the trends in social and economic organization are increasing the number of families whose resources are so low as to exclude them from even the minimum standards of living. Furthermore, the roles of individual family members, particularly women, have changed and require new responses from social programmes. Governments for the most part adopt pragmatic attitudes and responses to the family and its needs. At different times the family can be viewed as subversive or as a force for social and political stability, and it can become a battleground for opposing ideologies. Alternatively, states can see the family as the locus of national cultural values in times of external threat, or turn to the family when social spending is being reduced. Normally, most states tend to give the family low priority and regard rhetorical statements about the family being the basic unit of society as satisfactory proof of their commitment.

States are actively interventionist in legislating on marriage and divorce, contraception and abortion, school entry and leaving ages and compulsory vaccination programmes, but when it comes to practical and emotional care for family members, a different picture emerges. Almost all states operate on the premiss that families are responsible for caring for children, the sick and the elderly. This premiss usually assumes that women provide the care and that men, and maybe women, provide the cash. Social and economic institutions tacitly assume a traditional family structure and division of labour, and also that women mainly but men also will continue to perform a range of essential social functions within the community.

PRIORITIES OF THE LABOUR MARKET

When governments need to increase women's participation in the formal labour force they are more inclined to adopt pro-family measures, such as maternity rights or improved child care services. In the early 1980s the Cyprus government faced a labour shortage: it wanted to attract more women into the formal workforce and to encourage part-time workers to become full-time, while at the same time maintaining or increasing the population growth rate. It guaranteed working women's right to maternity leave, and expanded and improved public and private sector child care services to allow women 'to combine their traditional role of wife and mother with economic activity', and succeeded in attracting more women workers. Employers, however, continued discriminatory recruitment and employment practices.

At present in many Northern countries the low birth rate and the shortage of young workers have made employers and governments keen to recruit women; thus there is much more talk about child care services. Labour shortages can have the opposite effect: pro-natalist policies can result in the sanctification of the family and the consequent contraction of women's rights. The Malaysian government's current policy of increasing

the population from 15 to 70 million in 115 years, by each woman having five children, may have negative consequences for women's rights.[10] Women's right to work in the formal economy is not secure: when unemployment and labour surpluses occur, state policies are reversed rapidly, as happened in the former USSR under *perestroika* and in East Germany on unification.

In 1981, the International Labour Conference adopted a new convention, the Workers with Family Responsibilities Convention (No. 156) and a new Workers with Family Responsibilities Recommendation (No. 165); this was the first time at the international level that child care was considered to be the concern of men as well as women. Convention 156 requires the 127 member states of the International Labour Organization to:

[M]ake it an aim of national policy to enable persons with family responsibilities who are engaged or wish to engage in employment to exercise their right to do so without being subject to discrimination and, to the extent possible, without conflict between their employment and family responsibilities. (Article 3)

Recommendation 165, which accompanies the Convention, elaborates the kind of measures which could be taken: reduced working time and overtime; flexible working schedules; parental leave of absence in the period immediately following maternity leave; and protection of part-time workers. It emphasizes choice in the provision of child care. As of August 1992, nineteen countries had ratified Convention 156.

MATERNITY LEAVE Maternity leave is one of women's most basic protections and is a recognition of the importance of full-time mother care in infants' early months. It is an interesting case study of governments' commitment to women and to the family, and highlights the situation of millions of

PHOTO: WORLD COUNCIL OF CHURCHES/PETER WILLIAMS

Families with more than two children are rare in Norway and other Nordic countries.

women workers who are outside the formal employment sector. Maternity provision, in theory, guarantees women a continuing source of income and security of employment while enabling them to care for their newborn infants; but it is far from being a universally recognized or enforceable right. The Maternity Protection Convention, the first international standard, was adopted in 1919 and revised in 1952.

Most countries, worldwide, have legalized women's right to maternity leave. Each national situation is unique and often the legislation is a maze of eligibility exclusions, varying from levels and length of social security contributions to a minimum period of full-time employment. In Britain, for example, two years' uninterrupted employment is the minimum condition; some countries, such as Denmark, extend maternity entitlements without precondition.

Maternity cash benefits are paid in most countries, but not in the USA; the level varies from full- to half-wage replacement. Sometimes the employer pays and is then reimbursed by the state; social security services may pay directly to the woman. The average length of maternity leave is around twelve weeks. In countries where a period of six months to one year is allowed, payments are invariably reduced for the latter part of the leave. In Kenya, for example, women are allowed two months but forfeit their annual leave for that year. Nordic countries have the most progressive legislation. In Sweden, the parental leave during which parental benefit is provided is in total 450 days. For the first 12 months the benefit paid by public insurance is 90 per cent of wages, and it is a fixed daily rate of 60 Swedish krona for the following 90 days. A maximum of 360 days' leave may be taken by one parent only. In Finland, permitted leave is 263 weekdays, 105 of these being allocated to the mother. This period is extended by 60 days if more than one child at a time is born into the family. Adoptive parents are entitled to a maximum of 234 weekdays' leave. Parental benefit is in the range of 70 to 80 per cent of wages and is paid from public insurance.

During maternity leave, women are

usually protected against dismissal and entitled to return to the position they held before their leave, or a comparable one. Breast-feeding breaks, though usually unpaid, are the norm in the South, but not universally permitted in the North; the average time allowed tends to be two periods of half an hour each.

Maternity leave provisions, whether liberal or restricted, benefit only comparatively few women. In many countries, provision is rife with discrimination: for example, exclusion of part-time workers and of those in small workplaces. Most women in part-time, temporary or informal sector work do not benefit from maternity legislation. Domestic workers in most countries have no protection. Farmers and agricultural workers throughout Africa, Asia and Latin America usually work until the day of delivery and, except in rare cases, return to work immediately afterwards. All women in the informal sector, and home-workers, are likewise unprotected. Factory workers in many Southern countries are denied their statutory maternity rights unless it suits their employer; in the North it is not unknown for women to lose their formal sector job when they become pregnant regardless of the legal situation. Much depends on the national government's willingness both to extend its legislation to all sectors of employment and then to enforce it.

In a society that aims to enable men as well as women to fulfil their family responsibilities, it would be logical to promote paternity leave and a wide range of parental leave. In many countries, men commonly take some days off, officially or otherwise, at the time of their child's birth. Parental leave is a longer time that either parent can take off work to care for a young child. Where extended parental leave is allowed, however, social attitudes and the workplace ethos can discourage fathers from availing themselves of it, although increasing numbers of men now do.

CHILD CARE FACILITIES Good child care facilities, essential to allow parents to combine family and workplace responsibilities, are nonexistent in some countries and in chronically short supply in most. Even where governments are rhetorically committed, they frequently fail to allocate the necessary funds. The low priority ascribed to child care services stems from reservations about women's role in the workplace and the ill-founded notions that children must be cared for only by their mothers. Low priority is allocated to these facilities because child care is seen as women's responsibility, because women have consistently shown their capacity to cope, and because by and large they are marginalized within decision-making processes.

Reorganization of working practices seems to be one important part of the solution to child care needs. Shorter working hours could allow women and men with young children to share responsibility for child care. At present, however, part-time work can result in part-time rights and benefits, or none at all, and in effect can give employers greater flexibility to hire and fire. COFACE argues that it would be logical to take advantage of high unemployment (in Europe for example) to vary the distribution and flexibility of work time to better combine it with family, professional, and social obligations. It concludes: 'The choice is much more a political one than an economic one: should a non-profitable but vital activity – family life – be taken into account when organizing the division of economically profitable activity?'[11]

SOCIAL SECURITY Families need a positive response from state structures in many other areas. The way economies and societies are currently organized necessitates systems of social security to complement and facilitate family solidarity, such as financial support for families on low incomes

PHOTO: JENNY MATTHEWS

Provision of communal day-care is essential for working parents. Free day-care programme for under-sixes established by the Sandanista government at a tobacco factory in Esteli, Nicaragua.

or without a source of income, or minimum old age pensions. There is also a second layer of entitlements related to employment and salary levels, such as occupational pension schemes. The social security systems developed in most Western European countries since 1945 were founded on the concept of general solidarity: the better-off in society would assist those in need. Generally, most workers in the public and private sectors are well protected,[12] and social security payments, although rarely adequate, provide a safety net for many individuals and families with low or no income. In most Southern countries social security systems are limited in scope and frequently benefit only those in formal sector employment. In Africa, for example, less than 10 per cent of the population is employed in the formal sector. In Latin America, the situation is only slightly better: by and large the systems have evolved with industrialization and are closely linked to economic activity usually in urban areas. In

most countries less than 25 per cent of the formal labour force is eligible for some benefits.[13] The reality is that in Southern countries very few women are covered by social security, partly due to the sex segregation of many occupations and partly because most women in both rural and urban areas work in the informal sector.

In Northern countries many factors can reduce entitlement to such benefits as exist: they are frequently linked to past employment and length of residence; married women not in paid employment are perceived as dependants and are excluded from receiving social security in their own right separate from their husbands' circumstances. At present, pension-splitting in the case of divorce is mandatory in only two countries, Canada and Germany. People who are unemployed or have irregular or unstable employment, a situation in which many women with children find themselves, receive less social security protection. 'In most [Northern] countries social legislation still makes little allowance for the atypical forms of paid work in which . . . particularly large numbers of women are employed.' Shorter hours worked in part-time employment can exclude workers from social security benefits. Furthermore, as women's salaries are usually lower than men's their social security protection from schemes linked to occupational activity and salary level is less.

Some progress has been made in recent years in some European countries to grant entitlements to women, to offset interruptions in work for family reasons in the form of social security and pension 'credits', and to compensate for time spent caring for children. In Sweden, the parent's pension account is credited with one year's income for any interruption lasting six months in any one year for time spent caring for a child or children under three years.[15] Similar policies have been adopted in France and elsewhere. Such credits should be made available to women and men.

Certain groups within each society require specific policy and practical responses. One-parent families, women-maintained households especially, the elderly poor and elderly women, particularly those living alone, need various types of support. Allowances have been allocated in several countries but the sums involved are rarely sufficient to raise those concerned above the poverty line.

Two parallel steps are needed:

- **the elimination of the causes of women's inequality in the labour market;**

- **the provision of a safety net for women in precarious financial situations.**

Social security systems have come under scrutiny in the last decade or so; this is inspired partly by the economic crisis but also by changing political climates in several countries. COFACE is concerned about the possibility of a more fundamental reassessment, or rejection, of the principle of social protection systems based on the concept of general solidarity. If this principle is questioned, COFACE warns, it is a short step to guaranteeing only minimal social protection to those who 'really need it' and assuming all other costs will be met by family solidarity or private insurance.[16]

There is already a growing redirection in policy towards privatized services and community care. The shift from institutional to community care stems from both a move to contain costs and the intention to enable older persons, for example, to live independently in their own homes for as long as possible.[17] While it is desirable for many reasons that older people, and young and old people with physical or psychological disabilities remain in their community, in the absence of the necessary support services, 'community care' in effect means 'women-care'. The gap between the availability of services and the ability of the elderly to lead independent lives seems to be widening.[18]

This same trend towards privatization of services either to the family or to commercial or voluntary organizations is at the heart of the structural adjustment programmes being implemented in many Southern countries (see Chapter 6). These programmes are likewise based on a notion of the elasticity of women's time, energy and goodwill.

The ideal family policy would guarantee each family unit, and each individual within it, a satisfactory standard of living, thus enabling them to fulfil their economic, social, educational and cultural family roles. All family units must have this guarantee regardless of the parents' marital status, class, race, nationality or sexual orientation, or of whether the children are raised in a single, two- or multi-parent situation.

CONCLUSION ☐ Changes have taken place: formal equality is enshrined in the

have been taken to improve the access of all girls and women to the resources, (such as education, training and health care) and to the decision-making that are essential both for their own and their families' well-being. But progress is slow and other priorities consistently precede both women's rights and family welfare. Experience has shown that whilst mass education, formal sector employment and equality legislation all play a key role in diminishing discrimination, they have not brought about a significant shift in the control and use of resources.

Skrede identified two stages in the process towards gender equality: the symbolic, which involves establishing a public policy for equal status between the sexes; and the materialistic, which involves integrating gender issues into public policy in general. Norway, in her view, has reached the symbolic stage, but the materialistic stage will be far more difficult as it means not only access to equal rights (no discrimination) but also major changes in terms of redistribution and reallocation of resources. She sums up the process towards gender equality as follows: 'A great deal has been achieved and at the same time very little is achieved.'[19]

Four elements seem to be essential to bring about fundamental change: constitutional and legal reforms to guarantee equality between women and men; public education to inform and change attitudes; the social, economic and political infrastructure to make equality a reality; and strong women's organizations to set the agenda, monitor progress and press for the necessary redefinition of values and redistribution and reallocation of resources.

Changes in social legislation and policies are vital for removing gender inequalities and for supporting families. Yet despite the major changes that have taken place in most societies, social policies and programmes are still largely based on outmoded concepts and family models. Child care facilities, parental leave, pensions, and benefits for the

unemployed, single parents and the disabled (granted on the basis of an individual right to social protection rather than a system based on family situation) are the essential infrastructure to the removal of gender-based biases in society and the support of families. Equally important is education on sexuality, health and family planning, child development, conflict management, and the reorganization of paid work. Communication and coordination between all the institutions that affect the family – social services, employers, schools and religious institutions – are essential.

It is within the reach of most states and communities to build adequate and appropriate social services; it is a matter of priorities. For the South, this capacity is severely diminished but not eliminated by repayments on external debts and the rigours of structural adjustment programmes. It is impossible for countries ripped apart by military strife or external aggression to deliver social services; it must be recognized, however, that in many instances it is the very existence of extreme inequalities that leads to strife. What is a government's primary objective if not to manage the state's resources and relationships in such a way as to ensure the well-being of all its people? Paltiel argues that the whole concept of the relationship between the economy and society has to be reversed:

The concept was that society had to sustain the economy and not *vice versa*. Of course, we need to build healthy economies, but we need them to sustain healthy, productive and solidary societies, wherein people enjoy basic security and safety as well as freedom to act.[20]

Edgar maintains that in order to formulate adequate family policies we must look at all social policies in terms of their impact on family well-being and 'not permit a false dichotomy to be drawn between "economic" policies and "social" policies'.

The language of discussion thus needs to move towards a more explicit public-private 'partnership' model of family support, so that responsibility for family survival and well-being is seen not as that of the private family alone, but also that of the wider community and the government, employers and other institutions whose actions impinge on family life. Too often 'the public' side is conceptualized as the state welfare bureaucracy. Not often enough is attention paid to the damaging structures of work, urban design and schools which could and should be more 'family-friendly'.[21]

1. Asia Pacific Forum on Women, Law and Development, *Forum News*, Vol. 3, No. 1, December 1990.

2. A. M. Succar, 'Case study on Peru', paper prepared for the Inter-regional Seminar on CEDAW, Athens, 23-27 January 1989.

3. V. Somswasdi, 'Women in the Constitution of Thailand: a far-fetched hope for equality', in *Women's Legal Position in Thailand*, Chaingmai University, Women's Studies Programme, Faculty of Social Sciences, May 1991, pp. 1-19.

4. G. Kelkar, 'Violence against women: an understanding of responsibility' in M. Davies (ed.), *Third World, Second Sex 2*, London, Zed Books, 1987.

5. M. Molyneux, 'Family reform in socialist states: the hidden agenda', *Feminist Review*, No. 21, 1985, pp. 47-64.

6. E. Jelin (ed.), *Women and Social Change in Latin America* (English version), London, Zed Books, 1990.

7. N. Aguiar, 'Introducing Alternatives', in Development Alternatives for Women in a New Era (DAWN), *Alternatives Volume II: women's visions and movements*, Rio de Janeiro, DAWN, 1991.

8. COFACE (Confederation of Family Organizations in the European Community), *Families in a Frontier-free Europe*, 1989.

9. J. Moerman, 'The family today and its prospects for tomorrow', paper presented to a meeting in Budapest, 28 August 1987.

10. H. L. Chee, 'Babies to order: official population policies in Malaysia and Singapore', in B. Agarwal (ed.), *Structures of Patriarchy: the state, the community and the household*, New Delhi and London, Kali for Women and Zed Books, 1988.

11. COFACE, p. 7.

12. A. M. Brocas, A. M. Caillouz and V. Oget, *Women and Social Security: the progress towards equality of treatment*, Geneva, ILO, 1990, p. 37.

13. M. Folbre, 'Mothers on their own: policy issues for developing countries', unpublished paper for the Population Council and the International Center for Research on Women, 1991.

14. Brocas et al.

15. Ibid., p. 91.

16. COFACE (Confederation of Family Organizations in the European Community), *Families and Social Protection*, 1989.

17. M. Coopmans, A. Harrop and M. Hermans-Huiskes, *The Social and Economic Situation of Older Women in Europe*, Brussels, Commission of the European Communities, 1989, quoted in *Ageing International*, June 1990.

18. Ibid.

19. K. Skrede, 'Approaching the second stage? Gender issues in public policy: Norwegian experiences and challenges', paper presented to a UNESCO Meeting of Experts for the European Region to examine 'ways in which women may exert a more effective influence on the action of public authorities and decision-making processes', Oslo, 5-9 February 1990.

20. F. L. Paltiel, 'Education to identity and solidarity', in *Report of the Fourth International Working Seminar on The Caring Society in a Threatened Economy, 11-15 July 1990*, Institute for Study in Salzburg, 1990, pp. 41-50.

21. D. Edgar, 'Conceptualizing family life and family policies', paper prepared for the Second Ad Hoc Inter-agency Meeting on the International Year of the Family, Vienna, 5-6 March 1992.

8 CONCLUSION: HOPE IN CHANGE

I n my work I have experienced the great unfolding power of human beings who, when they are given the opportunity and freedom to analyze their situation and to take corrective action, will always come up with most realistic solutions. It is time we took people seriously, put them first and let them act![1]

THE LATE-TWENTIETH-CENTURY WORLD is a harsh place for individuals and families to live, love, work and rest in. Civil or military conflict is rife in some regions. In some countries the use of military might to suppress any progressive movement is commonplace and the abuse of human rights is routine. The arms trade feeds this militarization and diverts precious resources from essential social and economic programmes. The narcotics and pornography industries thrive on undermining human dignity, whilst in the eyes of some, sexual and physical violence against girls and women remains acceptable.

The economic and environmental crises have far-reaching effects and exacerbate existing inequalities in access to resources. Extreme poverty is in itself a form of violence. Neo-liberal thinking is dominating debate and action on development strategy. Economic liberalization, as espoused by the international financial institutions, is applied selectively: Southern countries are to remove trading barriers, deregulate their economies, cut subsidies and public expenditure, and privatize services like education or health care; Northern countries continue to protect their industries and set up trading blocs with preferential terms.

The glorification of the market as the final judge of economic efficiency and the fount of equal opportunity for all has reached new heights. But the market is a blunt instrument in the hands of the powerful and wealthy. Elson writes that for several reasons markets, no matter how competitive, are not fully adequate instruments for securing economic democracy; markets give more say to those with most purchasing power, for example, and cannot take account of activities and effects that have no price, such as unpaid family and community labour.[2]

Since those who champion economic liberalization also want to reduce the role of the state in social affairs, they emphasize the family's responsibility to cater for all the needs of its members. But there is a fundamental contradiction: the personal qualities valued by the marketplace – competitiveness, individualism and opportunism – are diametrically opposed to those qualities necessary for family solidarity. The marketplace concept that everything has its price is, of course, never applied to unpaid work.

The economic and social essentials for survival and well-being are no longer available to millions of women, men and children. They are marginalized from land use or ownership, from employment, from even the most basic education, healthcare and housing, and from any say in the running of their countries. The previous progress made in improving literacy, infant and child mortality rates and in the numbers of girls and boys receiving full-time education is in jeopardy. It is difficult for family members to act together as a cohesive, effective and educative unit of mutual solidarity when, for example, they have only meagre resources or when circumstances compel them to live and work far apart.

The fact that most families still manage to survive is due in no small measure to the energy, initiative and fearlessness of their women members, who do not spare themselves in seeking to ensure the survival of their children and other dependants.

THE SOUTH/NORTH GAP The late twentieth century is characterized by a widening gap between the poverty of three-quarters of the world's people and the relative wealth of the minority. Although the overall picture remains one of over-consumption in the North and under-consumption in the South, we cannot disregard the existence of significant social groups in the South who possess great wealth, and significant social groups in the North who live in poverty, perpetuated in both cases by gender, class and race differences. This over-consumption is not just in the area of food and natural resources, but also in the concentration of economic wealth and power, scientific and technological advances, education and basic services. The disparity in power and access to resources between women and men is particularly striking in all countries. Most families' human and economic resources and their relationships to the social and natural environment are affected by this distortion.

At the level of the family's productive and reproductive roles, the South/North disparity is intense. A typical family in the North has a low reproductive capacity: few women in their reproductive years, fewer children, greater numbers of dependent elderly, but good access to consumer goods and productive assets. By contrast, a typical family in the South has a high reproductive capacity: more women of child-bearing age, more children and potential workers, fewer elderly dependants, but extremely limited access to productive resources.[3]

TRENDS AND DIFFERENCES Undeniably, families in most countries are facing difficulties. It is possible to differentiate between those difficulties directly linked to the external economic and political situation of the countries in which families live, and those problems that are due more to how families are structured and to their internal relations. Problems such as the growing numbers of very young children living and working on the streets, child prostitution or drug abuse stem directly from the poverty and powerlessness in which millions of families find themselves and which on their own they are unable to combat. In the North, a minority of families are incapable of functioning at all. The generation of adults whose own childhood was marked by broken relationships and poverty are now parents. Many have been so poorly socialized themselves, they are incapable of adequately caring for and socializing their own children. The result is a rising generation of young people alienated from society.

Economic developments have been accompanied by social change led by new attitudes and behaviour. The large increase in migration from rural to urban areas in the past few decades with the ensuing dispersal of family members and the growth of megacities has led to new behaviour. Other important social changes include the following: women's growing independence; rising divorce and separation rates; dislocation of many men from their families. Within a few decades the norms of social behaviour have altered significantly in most societies. The speed at which these social changes have taken place has created insecurity and instability in family life. Some new family forms have emerged which may or may not be temporary. Women-maintained families are multiplying; increasing numbers of children have non-residential or visiting fathers whilst some have two homes, one with each parent.

Relations between women and men are changing in many countries. Inevitably, with greater educational and employment opportunities and the availability of contraception, women question the hierarchical structure of the family and the unequal

119

power relations within it. This has opened up some new choices in ways of living, loving, parenting and working. The growth of women's organizations has been significant in this process. Women are seeking more egalitarian family structures; they are not rejecting the family, and certainly not their families.

With greater longevity and the growing numbers of older women and men, many of whom are active, skilled and energetic, it would be just and sensible to find new ways of ensuring that older people play a central role in our societies. There are already, for example, a myriad of community support initiatives which could be taken as good practice and replicated elsewhere. All that is needed is a positive change in society's perceptions about older people.

The family will continue to be the basic unit of society and it is clear now that families will take many forms. The importance to individuals of kin and conjugal family bonds and relations is undeniable: the family grouping offers, potentially, spontaneous solidarity, emotional support and protection as well as a comprehensive reference system in dealings with others. Although individual family members know that the reality of family life does not always match the ideal or the potential, for the most part this does not diminish their commitment to the ideal itself.

The family as an institution is constantly evolving and always has shown itself able to respond to changes brought about by external forces. It is now facing a challenge from within from its women members. To date, many men have not reacted well: the challenge has heightened tensions between women and men and often aroused hostility. It has also brought new enlightenment to many men already uncomfortable in the straitjacket with which social and economic organization has confined their emotions and humanity. Families need to develop new egalitarian and democratic forms. Women's

equality and its full acceptance by men is central to this.

The new family realities have yet to be fully reflected in family policy or in the responses of society's institutions. The state has a crucial role in empowering women and men to fulfil their family responsibilities. Women must be enabled to carry out their responsibilities without jeopardizing their own well-being and personal development; men must be encouraged and enabled to commit greater time, energy and labour to family matters. Through integrated social and economic policies, through legislation and the allocation of resources, states can support families. Key areas are equal rights legislation, education, child care facilities, the reorganization of paid work, health and social services and action against violence. As UNICEF argues: 'Not to assist the family is, in fact, to do harm to its individual members, and to disregard their rights to benefit from a care-giving and convivial family life.'[4] A necessary corollary to this is to value the vital social functions of caring, socializing, parenting and day-to-day human maintenance that is carried on within families.

Positive action at the international level is a second necessary corollary. This involves devising alternative development strategies for the North as well as for the South, which start from a gender perspective and recognize reproduction as well as production, and are built upon a foundation of respect for human rights.

Women's organizations and other social movements are taking the lead in pressing for these changes, which would enable families to function well.

The international community, through such initiatives as the International Year of the Family, could play a leading role in building a favourable climate and the necessary political will to allow families the three things they need most: value, equality, and support.

WE, WOMEN

Cornelia Frettlöh wrote this poem in
1985 when she was living in Barbados.
She now lives in Germany.

The flood
    of oppression and hunger
The flood
    of starvation and war
The flood
    of misery and deforestation
The flood
    of chemical suicide and radiation
The flood
    of injustice and exploitation
The flood
    of malnutrition and poverty
The flood
    of all human disasters
The new flood
    caused by man

Who will stop it?
Who will build the ark?
Who if not we?
We
    the experts
    of discrimination and sorrow
We,
    the experts
    of inequality and pain
We,
    the experts
    of suffering and sacrifice
We,
    the viceroys for one decade
    losers for centuries

We,
    obtainers of rights on paper
    receivers of prejudice every day
We,
    who will not be contented with
    becoming an engineer
We,
    who will not be deluded
    by the magic of participation

You who are too busy
    with power and violence
    with build-up of weapons
    with maintaining the status quo
You who even think of bringing
    eternal death to the stars and the
      moon
    we don't want to become share-
      holders
    of your monster of a future
We,
    who are pregnant
    with a vision of the future
We,
    who are pregnant
    with a vision of hope
We,
    who are pregnant
    with a dream of Utopia
We,
    who else if not we
    will build the ark.

Source: *Cafra News*, Vol. 4, No. 2,
June–August 1990.

---

1. S. Nyoni, 'Women, environment and development in Zimbabwe', in *Report of the Women, Environment and Development Seminar, 7 March 1989*, London, Women's Environmental Network and War on Want, 1989, pp. 25–7.
  2. D. Elson, 'Gender issues in development strategies', paper presented to the Seminar on the Integration of Women in Development, Vienna, 9–11 December 1991.
  3. Isis/WICCE, personal communication, 1991.
  4. UNICEF, *Introduction to Some Guiding Principles on the Family*, 1989.

ANNEX I

A GUIDE TO EDUCATION AND ACTION

IN THIS ANNEX, the UN-NGO Group on Women and Development suggests ways in which this book could be used by groups that wish to deepen their understanding of the issues surrounding women and the family as a prelude to advocacy and action.

Because of the diversity among readers of this series, not all the suggestions will be relevant to every group. You may be using this book in a development education group, or in connection with an action programme in your community. Group members may all be women, or women and men, or older and younger people. You may be in an academic setting with formal classes or in an informal discussion group. You may belong to an established international agency or NGO, or to an emerging women's group.

Whatever your situation and your objective, we hope that some of these ideas can be adapted to your needs or that you will be able to suggest other, better and more appropriate ideas. Each group must come to its own conclusions about its priority issues and opportunities for action.

The phrase 'your area' is used below loosely to mean the locality or region in which your group operates; your area of concern or interest; and your sphere of action. In short, it refers to whatever constitutes your group's 'arena of action'.

SUGGESTIONS AND QUESTIONS

1. Describe and discuss the family structure in your area. What are the main functions of the family, and how has it changed in the lifetime of your family? Identify the main causes of change, for example migration, changing attitudes, poverty, educational opportunities. Which changes have been beneficial to women and why? Which have been negative and why? What changes would your group like to see in family structure? How could these changes be achieved?

2. Describe and discuss the division of labour within the family in your area, between women and men of all ages and between girl and boy children. Include all kinds of work: caring, preparation of food and domestic work as well as economic activities carried on within the family. Does the division of labour pose particular problems for women family members? If so, what are these and how could change be achieved?

3. Time-use studies are an illuminating way of finding out exactly how women, and men, spend each day, how many hours are spent caring for children, cooking, fetching food, water or other essentials, sleeping, resting and on recreational pursuits. Members of your group could start with their own daily lives and record how they spend their time, and then add up the amount of time spent in each activity. Next, your group could try to assess how families and the wider society value caring and domestic work and what determines this value. How could this value be increased? The group may then wish to organize a time-use study in your area.

4. Review chapters 2 to 5 and select a few key issues that are most important in your area or to the members of your group, or those where you have the best opportunities for taking action and bringing about change. These could include: the age of marriage; health care; breast-feeding; issues related to

employment, such as maternity and parental leave; family planning; abortion; child care; caring for elderly family members; school attendance and school leaving age; teenage pregnancy; education for family life; single parenthood; the law on maintenance, divorce or inheritance; social security; housing; violence. The group may define issues these chapters do not include which are more important to them and which require action.

5. Your group could find out all the information it can in relation to the key issue/s it has selected. This could include information about local or national government policy and services, relevant legislation, the work of women's organizations, statistics and recent research. It should then be possible to identify some specific areas in which policy changes would greatly improve family life and women's position in the family.

6. There are several in-depth studies in the book which could provide a valuable starting point for group discussions, for example, 'Marriage in Eritrea' and 'Women, sexuality and the family' in Chapter 2, 'An alternative vision of day care' in Chapter 3, 'Domestic workers and family life in Mexico', 'Maintenance for women and children in Southern Africa', 'Single parents in Korea' in Chapter 4.

7. Older women and men can face particular problems: they can be highly respected and cared for but can also be neglected and face isolation and poverty. Describe and discuss the situation of older women and then of older men in your area. What particular problems do each face? How could these problems be tackled?

ORGANIZING A SEMINAR

Several of the suggestions below could be the basis for all or part of a seminar organized by your group. The seminar guidelines below, drawn up by the Asian and Pacific Development Centre, Kuala Lumpur, have been found very useful by many groups.

1. Be sure about the purpose of the seminar.

2. Organize speakers/experts well in advance to give them time to prepare for the seminar and their papers on particular topics.

3. Arrange advance media coverage if you wish to have the purpose of the seminar made publicly known. Invite the media to cover the seminar if you want the message and outcome made known to a wider audience.

4. Select a skilled chairperson who can gauge when to adjourn or to break up into group discussions.

5. Identify resource people who can act as group discussion leaders and rapporteurs who will write down the main ideas. In the absence of skilled rapporteurs some advance training is recommended to ensure that group discussions are adequately reflected in the plenary session or in the final report.

6. Select participants according to the objectives of the seminar. Ask them to bring their experiences in written form, pictures or on tapes, for use in the workshop sessions.

7. Choose an environment appropriate to the seminar topic, for example, at the village level if related to the rural poor.

8. Provide basic facilities and ensure

adequate working space as well as secretarial and clerical support for participants.

9. Consider the use of audio-visual material – tapes, slides, charts – as tools to provide the focus for discussion.

10. Have a definite schedule prepared to present to participants and stress that the goals be achieved within that time scale.

11. As an introduction, arrange an informal session to allow participants to become acquainted. This will encourage a relaxed atmosphere and free exchange of views.

12. At the commencement of the seminar, make the purpose clear to the participants.

13. The organizer should have some idea of the anticipated outcome and be prepared to intervene and state this.

14. Do not overtax participants, particularly on the first day. Allow adequate time for private study and social activities.

15. To maintain interest and alertness, plan a range of approaches – practical exercises, simulated games, 'brainstorming', breaking into small groups, etcetera.

16. Ensure ongoing evaluation and feedback to participants.

17. Allow flexibility according to what evolves in the course of the seminar and do not rule out any alternatives.

18. Try to overcome cultural barriers through observation and sensitivity.

19. Follow up the seminar with analysis and evaluation.

A TYPICAL SEMINAR PROGRAMME

Seminars can vary in length from a few hours to a few days. The Seminar Plan (pp. 127) is for a typical three-day seminar, but could be adapted for seminars of between one and five days. The plan assumes that the seminar will focus on one of the key issues in this book.

It is important first to clarify the objective of the seminar. It could be, for example, to increase awareness of a particular issue among your organization or other target audiences; or it could be to draw the problem to the attention of decision-makers in order to bring about changes in laws, policies or attitudes that would eliminate or mitigate the problem. An example here could be one of the following: more educational opportunities for girls and women; better sex education in schools; education for family life; appropriate family planning services; the extension of maternity leave to employment sectors not currently covered; police training on dealing with family violence.

The seminar plan would be appropriate for a national or a regional seminar with about thirty participants, plus about four or five resource persons and staff of the organizing agency. The seminar could be organized by a women's organization or national NGO. The expected outcome is a plan of action which can be taken up by each group within their area, such as a local women's group, trade union branch, national agency, health workers' association, lawyers, religious group, policy-makers and so on.

The programme comprises plenary sessions, to include all participants, as well as smaller workshops in which each member can speak, topics can be discussed in depth, and detailed plans of action agreed.

In advance of the seminar it is important that each participant receives background papers setting out the important issues.

	DAY 1	DAY 2	DAY 3
MORNING	**Plenary session** Welcome – host organization Keynote speaker – overview of the issue Organizer – objectives of the seminar *Break* **Panel of speakers** on the root causes of the problem: ● cultural ● social ● economic ● political Questions and discussion	**Panel presentation** One or two speakers give examples of successful action in another area/country on same or related issue. Questions and discussion *Break* **Workshops** Brainstorming on ideas for action on the issue. This could include enlisting the support of other relevant organizations and/or influential people, requesting a meeting with the appropriate government official, seeking media coverage of the issue, planning a larger public event. *Break* Move on from brainstorming to an evaluation of ideas for action	**Workshops** Complete preliminary outline of plan of action. This could include specific objectives, timetable, division of labour, budget, sources of funds, representatives from each area, composition of steering committee, involvement of local community groups and organizations. *Break* **Workshops** Drafting of workshops' reports by rapporteurs, resource persons and other workshop members
AFTERNOON	**Workshops*** Small groups discuss the dimensions of the problem in their area/country and, where appropriate, examine differences on grounds of age, social group, ethnic group, religion, educational level and so on. *Break* Is the necessary information on government policy, existing legislation, the work of other organizations available? How much awareness exists now? * Each working group has one or more resource persons who can assist the discussion.	**Workshops** Begin to develop a preliminary plan of action and define: ● objectives ● actions required, what, where, when, how? ● who is responsible at each step? ● how to measure progress at each step. *Break* Continue work on plan of action.	**Plenary** Brief oral presentation of each workshop's report Outline written action plans distributed Questions and discussion *Break* **Final closing session** Summing-up Arrangements for follow-up and progress at different levels Close (Hand in questionnaire on evaluation of seminar)

Material from this book and others in this series could be useful in preparing these papers. In addition, each participant should receive a registration form to complete and return some weeks before the seminar. If there are workshops on different themes it is useful for planning purposes to ask participants to indicate in advance which workshops they would like to attend. Seminar participants should also be encouraged to bring materials relating to their organization's work, as well as publications, posters, photographs or cuttings for display.

In addition to the formal discussion sessions, time in the programme could be allotted for more general participation, such as role play, which can be a very lively and interesting way to highlight issues. Videos and other audio-visual materials should also be used as much as possible. For example, one hour after the evening meal could be set aside to watch a video on the seminar topic followed by a short informal discussion.

Organizers should prepare in advance a short seminar evaluation questionnaire for each participant to complete before they leave.

SUGGESTED PLAN FOR A SEMINAR

It is assumed that participants would arrive in the evening before the first day, in order to register and participate in an informal 'get acquainted' and information-sharing session.

ANNEX II

SELECTED

ORGANIZATIONS

American Association of Retired Persons, 601 E Street NW, Washington, DC 20049, USA

Asia Pacific Forum on Women, Law and Development, 9th Floor APDC Building, Pesiaran Duta, PO Box 12224, 50770 Kuala Lumpur, Malaysia

Asian Women's Association, Shibuya Coop 211, 14-10 Sakuragaok, Shibuya-ku, Tokyo 169, Japan

Awakening, Flat 3 No 1 Lane 1, Po-ai Road, Taipei, Taiwan

Centre for Women's Development Studies, B-43 Panchsheel Enclave, New Delhi - 110 017, India

Change, PO Box 824, London SE24 9JS, UK

Child Poverty Action Group, 1–5 Bath Street, London EC1V 9PY, UK

Confederation of Family Organizations in the European Community (COFACE), rue de Londres 17, 1050 Brussels, Belgium

Commission of the European Communities (CEC), Women and Development Office, DGVIII rue de la Loi 200, 1049 Brussels, Belgium

Committee for Asian Women, 57 Peking Road, 4/F Kowloon, Hong Kong

Commonwealth Secretariat, Women and Development Programme, Marlborough House, Pall Mall, London SW1Y 5HX, UK

Development Alternatives for Women in a New Era (DAWN), c/o WAND School of Continuing Studies, University of the West Indies, Pinelands, St Michael, Barbados

Division for the Advancement of Women, United Nations Department of Policy Co-ordination and Sustainable Development (UNDPCSD), PO Box 20, United Nations, New York, NY 10017, USA

FLACSO, Casilla 3213, Central de Casillas, Santiago, Chile

Flora Tristan Centro de la Mujer Peruana, Avenida Arenales 601, Lima, Peru

Foundation for Women's Health, 38 King Street, London WC2E 8JT, UK

Friends of Women Group, 1379/30 Soi Praditchai, Samsen-nai, Payathai, Bangkok 10400, Thailand

GABRIELA, PO Box 4386, Manila 2800, The Philippines

HelpAge International, St James Walk, London EC1R 0BE, UK

Inter-African Committee on Traditional Practices Affecting the Health of Women and Children, 147 rue de Lausanne, 1211 Geneva, Switzerland

International Center for Research on Women, 1717 Massachusetts Avenue NW, Suite 302, Washington, DC 20036, USA

International Council of Jewish Women, 110 Finch Avenue West, Suite 518, Downsview M3J QT2, Canada

International Council of Women, 13 rue Caumartin, 75009 Paris, France

International Council on Social Welfare, Koestlergasse 1/29, 1060 Vienna, Austria

International Federation on Ageing, 1919 K Street NW, Washington, DC, USA

International Federation of Social Workers, 33 rue de l'Athene, 1206 Geneva, Switzerland

International Federation of University Women, 37 quai Wilson, 1211 Geneva, Switzerland

International Labour Organization (ILO), 4 Chemin des Morillons, 1211 Geneva 22, Switzerland

International Organization of Consumer Unions, Emmastraat 9, 2595 EG Amsterdam, The Netherlands

International Organization of Consumer Unions, Regional Office for Asia and the Pacific, PO Box 1045, 10838 Penang, Malaysia

International Planned Parenthood Federation, Regent's College, Inner Circle, Regent's Park, London NW1 4NS, UK

International Women's Rights Action Watch, Humphrey Institute of Public Affairs, University of Minnesota, 301, 19th Avenue South, Minneapolis, MN 55455, USA

International Women's Tribune Center, 777 United Nations Plaza, New York, NY 10017, USA

Isis International, 85-A East Maya Street, Philamlife Homes, Quezon City, The Philippines

Korean Women's Development Institute, CPO Box 2267, Seoul, Korea

La Leche League International, 9616 Minneapolis Avenue, PO Box 1209, Franklin Park, Illinois 60131, USA

Manuela Ramos, Avenida Bolivia 921, Brena, Lima, Peru

Medical Women's International Association, Herbert Lewin Street 5, D-5000 Cologne 41, Germany

NGO/UN Cooperation Forum, Jalan Gatot Subroto Kav. 96, Jakarta 12790, Indonesia

NGO Committee on the Family/International Year of the Family, An der Hulben 1/15, A-1010 Vienna, Austria

Papua New Guinea Law Reform Commission, PO Box 4349, Boroko, Papua New Guinea

Population Council, One Dag Hammarskjold Plaza, New York, NY 10017, USA

Population Concern, 231 Tottenham Court Road, London W1P 9AE, UK

Self Employed Women's Association (SEWA), SEWA Reception Centre, Opp. Victoria Garden, Ahmedabad 380001, India

Social Development Index, 12 Pasaje de la Paz, Project 4, Quezon City, The Philippines

Status of Women Canada, 360 Albert Street, Ottawa, Ontario K1A 1C3, Canada

TAMWA Tanzania Media Women's Association, PO Box 6143, Dar es Salaam, Tanzania

United Nations Children's Fund (UNICEF), 3 United Nations Plaza, New York, NY 10017, USA

United Nations Children's Fund (UNICEF), Palais des Nations, 1211 Geneva 10, Switzerland

United Nations Development Programme (UNDP), One United Nations Plaza, New York, NY 10017, USA

United Nations Economic Commission for Europe (ECE), Palais des Nations, 1211 Geneva 10, Switzerland

United Nations Economic Commission for Latin America and the Caribbean (ECLAC), Casilla 179, Santiago, Chile

United Nations High Commission for Refugees, Palais des Nations, 1211 Geneva 10, Switzerland

United Nations Development Fund for Women (UNIFEM), 304 East 45th Street, 6th Floor, New York, NY 10017, USA

United Nations Non-governmental Liaison Service (NGLS), Palais des Nations, 1211 Geneva 10, Switzerland; 866 UN Plaza, Room 6015, New York, NY 10017, USA

United Nations Population Fund (UNFPA), 220 East 42nd Street, New York, NY 10017, USA

United Nations University, Toho Seimei Building, 15-1 Shibuya 2-chome, Shibuya-ku, Tokyo 150, Japan

World Health Organization (WHO), Avenue Appia, 1211 Geneva 27, Switzerland

Women and Development Europe (WIDE), c/o ICJP, 169 Booterstown Avenue, Dublin, Ireland

World Institute for Development and Economic Research (WIDER)/United Nations University (UNU), Annankatu 42 C, 00100 Helsinki 10, Finland

Women and Law in Southern Africa Research Project, Regional Office, PO Box UA 171, Union Avenue, Harare, Zimbabwe

Women and Pharmaceuticals/WEMOS, Post-box 4263, 1009 AG Amsterdam, The Netherlands

Women Living under Muslim Laws, BP 23, 34790 Grabels, France

Women's Development Collective, 43C Jalan SS 6/12, Kelana Jaya, 47301 Petaling Jaya, Selangor Danu Ehsan, Malaysia

Women's Global Network for Reproductive Rights, NWZ Voorburgwal 32, 1012 RZ Amsterdam, The Netherlands

Women's International League for Peace and Freedom, 1 rue de Varembe, CP 28, 1211 Geneva 20, Switzerland

Women's Resource and Research Center, Mary Knoll College Foundation Inc., Katipunan Parkway, Diliman, Quezon City, The Philippines

Working Women's Forum, 55 Bhimasena Garden Street, Mylapore, Madras 4, India

Women's World Banking (Ghana) Limited, PO Box 2989, Accra, Ghana

World Food Programme (WFP), Via Cristoforo Colombo 426, 1-00145 Rome, Italy

World University Service, 5 chemin Iris, 1216 Geneva, Switzerland

World Council of Churches, 150 route de Ferney, CP 2100, 1211 Geneva, Switzerland

BIBLIOGRAPHY

Agarwal, B. (ed.) (1988) *Structures of Patriarchy: state, community and household in modernising Asia*, New Delhi and London, Kali for Women and Zed Books.

Akhtar, Farida, (1992) *Depopulating Bangladesh: essays on the politics of fertility*, Dhaka, Bangladesh, UBINIG and Narigrantha Prabartana.

Antrobus, P. (1990) 'Strategies for change: design of programmes/plans', paper for the Commonwealth Caribbean Regional Meeting on Structural Adjustment, Economic Change and Women.

Armstrong A. K. (1992) *Struggling over Scarce Resources: women and maintenance in Southern Africa*, Women and Law in Southern Africa Research Trust Regional Report, Harare, University of Zimbabwe Publications.

Ashworth, G. (1985) *Of Violence and Violation: women and human rights*, London, Change.

Behnam, D. (1990) 'An international inquiry into the future of the family: a UNESCO project', *International Social Science Journal*, 126, November 1990, pp. 547–52.

Brocas, A. M., A. M. Cailloux and V. Oget, (1990) *Women and Social Security: the progress towards equality of treatment*, Geneva, ILO.

Bunch, C. and R. Carrillo, (1991) *Gender Violence: a development and human rights issue*, New Jersey, Center for Global Leadership.

COFACE (Confederation of Family Organizations in the European Community) (1985) *Women's Rights and Family Policy*.

COFACE (1989) *Families and Social Protection*.

Commission for Social Development (CSD) (1989) *World Social Situation, Including the Elimination of all Major Social Obstacles, Report on the World Social Situation, Thirty-first session*, Vienna, 13–22 March.

Commonwealth Expert Group on Women and Structural Adjustment (1989) *Engendering Adjustment for the 1990s*, London, Commonwealth Secretariat.

Commonwealth Secretariat Women and Development Programme (1992) *Confronting Violence: a manual for Commonwealth action*, London, Commonwealth Secretariat.

Convention on the Rights of the Child – drawn up at the World Summit for Children in 1989 and adopted by the UN General Assembly in 1989 and entered into force on 2 September 1990.

Convention on Elimination of all Forms of Discrimination against Women (CEDAW) – adopted and opened for signature, ratification and accession by the UN General Assembly on 18 December 1979.

DAWN (1991) *Alternatives Volume II: women's visions and movements*, Rio de Janeiro, Development Alternatives with Women in a New Era (DAWN).

Department of Women and Child Development (1991) *The Lesser Child: the girl in India*, Ministry of Human Resource Development, Government of India.

Dwyer, D. and J. Bruce (eds.) (1988) *A Home Divided: women and income in the Third World*, Stanford, Stanford University Press.

Elson, D. (1991) 'Gender issues in development strategies', paper presented to the Seminar on the Integration of Women in Development, Vienna, 9–11 December.

Finch, J. (1989) *Family Obligations and*

social change, Cambridge, UK, Polity Press.

Florez, C. E. (1990) The Demographic Transition and Women's Life Course in Colombia, Tokyo, UN University.

Folbre, N. (1991) 'Mothers on their own: policy issues for developing countries', Population Council and the International Center for Research on Women, unpublished paper.

Forbes Martin, S. (1992) Refugee Women, London, Zed Books.

Forward Looking Strategies for the Advancement of Women (1985) – adopted by the World Conference to Review and Appraise the Achievements of the UN Decade for Women.

FORWARD (1989) Report of the First National Conference on Female Genital Mutilation: unsettled issues for health and social workers in the UK, 1 February.

Gibson, M. J. (1991) 'West meets East at UN conference on ageing and the family – report on conference', Ageing International, June, pp. 33–42.

Gittins, D. (1985) The Family in Question: changing households and familiar ideologies, London, Macmillan.

Goldschmidt-Clermont, L. (1987) Economic Evaluation of Unpaid Household work: Africa, Asia, Latin America and Oceania, Geneva, ILO.

Hartman, B. (1987) Reproductive Rights and Wrongs: the global politics of population control and contraceptive choice, New York, Harper and Row.

ILO (1988) 'Work and family: the child-care challenge', Conditions of Work Digest, Vol. 7, No. 2.

Innocenti Declaration on the Protection, Promotion and Support of Breast-feeding, 1 August 1990.

Inter-Africa Committee on Traditional Practices Affecting the Health of Women and Children (IAC) (1990) Report of the Regional Conference on

Traditional Practices Affecting the Health of Women and Children, Addis Ababa, 19–24 November.

Jankanish, M. (1988) 'Responding to the child care needs of working parents: an overview', in ILO, Conditions of Work Digest, Vol. 7, No. 2.

Kitakysushu City Declaration from the UN Conference on Ageing in 1989.

Lewenhak, S. (1988) The Revaluation of Women's Work, London, Croom Helm.

McGowan, L. A. (ed.) (1990) The Determinants and Consequences of Female-headed Households, Notes from Seminar Series, Population Council and International Center for Research on Women.

Mies, M. (1986) Patriarchy and Accumulation on a World Scale: women in the international division of labour, London, Zed Books.

Moerman, J. (1987) 'The family today and its prospects for tomorrow', paper presented to a meeting in Budapest, 28 August 1987.

Moghadam, V. M. (forthcoming) 'Women and the changing family', in Social Change and Women in the Middle East, Boulder, CO, Lynne Rienner.

Network News. A Newsletter of the Global Link for Midlife and Older Women. Washington DC, American Association of Retired Persons.

Oppong, C. (1988) 'The effects of women's position on fertility, family organization and the labour market: some crisis issues', paper presented to the International Union for the Scientific Study of Population conference on 'Women's Position and Demographic Change in the Course of Development', Asker, Oslo.

Panos (1990) Triple Jeopardy; Women & AIDS, London, Panos Institute.

Papers Prepared for the Second Ad-Hoc Inter-Agency Meeting on the International

Year of the Family, Vienna, 5–6 March 1992.

Prieur, J. (1987) 'Introductory report to the International Conference on Families and Cultures', Paris, UNESCO, 4–5 December.

Rodda, A. (1991) *Women and the Environment*, London, Zed Books.

Royston, E. and S. Armstrong (eds.) (1989) *Preventing Maternal Deaths*, Geneva, WHO.

Sadik, Dr N. (1990) *Investing in Women: the focus of the 1990s*, New York, UNFPA.

Sadik, Dr N. (ed.) (1991) *Population Policies and Programmes: lessons learned from two decades of experience*, New York, UNFPA.

Sen, G. and C. Grown (1985) *Development Crisis and Alternative Visions: Third World women's perspectives*, New Delhi, DAWN.

Sennott-Miller, L. (1989) *Midlife and Older Women in Latin America and the Caribbean: a status report*, Washington, DC, American Association of Retired Persons and Pan American Health Organization.

Sparr, P. (ed.) (forthcoming) *Mortgaging Women's Lives: feminist critiques of structural adjustment*, London, Zed Books.

Tomaševski, K. (1993) *Women and Human Rights*, London, Zed Books.

Tinker, I. (ed.) (1990) *Persistent Inequalities*, Oxford, Oxford University Press.

Umfreville, M. (pseudonym) (1990) *$£XONOMYC$: an introduction to the political economy of sex, time and gender*, London, Change.

UNHCR (1989) 'Focus on the family', *Refugees*, No. 70, Geneva, November.

UNICEF (1989) *Introduction to Some Guiding Principles on the Family*.

UNICEF (1990) *The Girl Child: an investment in the future*, New York.

United Nations (1991) *The World's Women: trends and statistics 1970–1990*, New York, UN.

Vickers, J. (1991) *Women and the World Economic Crisis*, London, Zed Books.

Waring, M. (1989) *If Women Counted: a new feminist economics*, London, Macmillan.

Women and Pharmaceuticals Project (1991) 'Guidelines for the Distribution and Use of Fertility Regulating Methods'.

133

INDEX